YES,
YOU.

YES, YOU.

What if God could use exactly what
we've got to pull off something big?

written by

Willow Weston

Table of contents

The Collide Story

I remember walking into a counseling office over a decade ago because my pain was chasing me down. I had run into Jesus and had even been leading in ministry for years prior to walking in for help, but God was inviting me into a deeper healing than I had yet to receive and perhaps a higher calling than I had yet to understand. I walked in for guidance because my pain was leaking out in ways that scared me. I sat in that counselor's office and stared at her clock as she asked me the all too expected question: "So what brings you in here today?"

I had a run-in with Jesus Christ in that office that had nothing to do with the counselor. God gave me two words: wounded collision. He helped me to see that I was born into pain. I had collided with wounds that were never healed, and they wounded me and now I wounded others. Sometimes it seems like we are all bumping around, colliding and wounding each other. I sat in that room desperate for all of us to have a new kind of collision. My pain was crying out for it.

When I see Jesus, He collides with people and rather than wounding them, He leaves them more whole. God's Spirit showed up in that counseling office in a way that pierced the air. God invited me to see those who wounded me from His perspective rather than my own. God called me to enter people's brokennness, instead of running from it. God reminded me that He is, indeed, a God who wipes brokenness all over Himself. I was being invited to collide with Jesus in my brokenness and invite others to come along.

So, I walked out of that appointment holding a spiritual concept, but even more, I knew in my innards that I was being called to do something big with those two words. Soon afterwards a beautiful young college aged girl from church asked if I would mentor her. I wasn't feelin' like the mentoring type right about then. She said she wanted to learn more about Jesus. I invited her to get together and study the Bible and see what happens when Jesus collides with wounded people. She was excited, so excited, that she invited all her friends, because twenty some college women came knocking on my door.

We spent the next several years looking at Jesus colliding with people in the New Testament and as we did, He collided with us too. When Jesus restored the shriveled man's hand, He too, restored these college girls' shriveled self-esteems. When Jesus said to the woman caught in the act of adultery "go and sin no more", He too, said this to the young woman in my living room who had been caught stark naked in shame and Jesus set her free. When Jesus went out of His way to collide with the woman at the well who was going from man to man to man because she was so thirsty, Jesus too, met the college

girls in my living room and He gave them something to drink that quenched their parched living. Those twenty girls and I experienced a new kind of collision when we ran into Jesus, one that brought about wholeness.

Most of the girls had graduated and moved away from college. There were four girls left and they wanted to keep meeting. I prayed, and God said, "I am not into us four and no more Bible studies. It's time they teach the message." I was working as a college minster at the time and this idea came out of nowhere. I had a lot of other things on my plate, not to mention a full-time job, a husband and two kids. God handed us an opportunity to do something to impact lives that was beyond our understanding, but we had to act on His invitation. So, we did an experiment and that experiment led to what is now Collide, this ministry, that invites women of all ages, races, socioeconomic statuses, faith backgrounds, and life places to run into Jesus and as they do, they are forever transformed.

God took a story of pain and brokenness and turned it into this beautiful ministry we call Collide. We shape and craft **events**, conferences and retreats for thousands of women every year. We now have a **counseling program** assisting people who desire to walk towards healing in their life. We have a **mentoring program** where women are meeting in life changing intergenerational relationships, co-learning from one another. We have a **blog** that God is using to invite people all around the country to collide with Jesus. We have a **leadership and ministry development program** where we are inviting women to tap into God's purpose for their lives. We have a **church bridging program** partnering with many local churches in the hopes of inviting women to walk a bridge from our events into the local church, so they will keep colliding. We have an amazing **staff** of gifted passionate, fierce women who are giving their lives away for this mission. And this right here, in your hands, is our newest experiment, **Bible studies**, that we are creating and sharing in the hopes that more and more people will run into Christ.

I am continually amazed by this Jesus who shows up right smack dab in the midst of our mess and pain and walks us into healing and purpose. Collide has become a place, a community, a movement for many to run into Jesus just as they are. My hope is that in the same way God met me years ago when I most needed it, He too will meet you right where you find yourself. He is a God who collides...so get ready because He does incredible, big, mighty, miraculous, unimaginable things when you run into Him.

Willow Weston
founder and director of Collide

Collide Values

We value women colliding with Jesus and His teachings.

We value and encourage authenticity (telling our story as it really is).

We value recognizing brokenness, so it can be made whole.

We value the experience and support that comes from an intergenerational community of women of all ages, church backgrounds, life experiences, and faith stages.

We value teaching a theology that runs into the holistic parts of who we are, to encourage a healthy spirituality.

We value pushing towards growth and next steps to go further on one's journey with God.

We value challenging and building up ministers and allowing Collide to be their playground.

COLLIDE...
AN INTRODUCTION

Collide invites people of all ages, stages, experiences and faith backgrounds, as imperfect or broken as they may be on their journey, to authentically run into Jesus; as He collides with them, they are forever transformed.

Collide Mission

4

Who we are
and who we aren't

We are everyday chicks running into Jesus. This Bible study was written, researched and created by ordinary women of all ages, stages and backgrounds, desiring to know God. We have indigestion, PMS, anxiety, and bad hair days. We work jobs, serve on PTA boards, sit on church committees, coach sports and attempt to bless our neighbors. We have different skin colors, different generational experiences, different faith backgrounds and different economic statuses. We like Cheetos and red wine, candles, a good book and a walk on the beach. We get insecure and let fear get in our way sometimes. We battle and wrestle and pray and pray. We have bills to pay, kids to raise, relationships to reconcile and big dreams we'd like to see become reality. We are your neighbors, your friends, your everyday women.

We are not Bible scholars. We have not been to Seminary. We don't have a lot of letters after our name. We don't speak Hebrew or Greek. We are not all that impressive in "religious" circles. If you are looking for that kind of Bible study resource, there are so many great ones, and this might not be the one for you. We merely desire God and are mesmerized by Jesus. We want to learn, grow, study and be challenged and inspired by who God is and who He calls us to be. It is this desire that has led us to run into Jesus and to invite others to come along.

We are still in the midst of our story. We are in chapter 7, not at the end of the book. We have not "arrived." God's not done with us. What we think, feel, or believe might transform, morph, or reconstruct as God continues to collide with us. Who we are now and who we are becoming leaves room for us to be in process, to seek, to ask questions and to be God's kids. We believe God is the best Author and He writes the best story, and the story that He is writing in your life and ours is being written as we speak…and so we engage His best story and trust Him for chapter 8, chapter 9 and so on.

We don't have all the answers. We did not set out to write Bible studies because we think we have the Holy Bible nailed down. We do not think we know the answers to all the questions. We don't think we can solve age-old theological debates nor current hot button arguments. We don't think we are tighter with the Big Man upstairs and therefore can tell you all that you need to know. All we know for sure is that God is alive and well. He loves us, and He shows just how much He loves us in Jesus Christ. We know for sure that God desires to collide with us and when we do we are forever transformed. Because we don't have all the answers, we are okay with inviting you, our friends, to come with us as we collide with Jesus together. We don't feel the pressure to be know-it-alls, experts or professional

"Christians". Neither do we feel we need to provide you with all the answers, easy answers, formulas or a specified spiritual "track" that someone else prescribes. Let's together read, reflect, ruminate and respond. Let's not be afraid to have questions that lack easy answers. Let's not think God isn't big enough to handle our doubt. Let's not limit God to our confusion and misunderstandings. Let's not box Him in either. Let's just collide with Jesus and see what He will do.

We are broken. We have been abused, used, betrayed, judged, manipulated, beat down and lied to. We have skeletons in the closet, a long list of mistakes, shady pasts, paralytic fear and deep-seated bitterness we struggle with. We will not pretend we are something we aren't, and we won't ask you to either. We are not put together. We are not perfect. We are not immortal. We are not finished, fault-less or foolproof. We are not Christian poster children. We are sojourners, inviting you, in your brokenness, to walk alongside us in ours, and together, we will collide with Jesus and by His wounds, we will be made whole.

We aren't afraid to engage our brokenness or yours. We no longer want our past to determine our present. We know that the pain we have experienced can easily walk into all of our collisions and we want more than that for our lives. We want to see our wounds find their Healer. We want to see our pain experience redemption. We want to see our brokenness be used for good. We know there's no other way around pain than to allow Jesus to meet us in it. So, we let Him. We sit in discomfort, we remember, we grieve, we cry, we forgive, we get angry and cry out like the Psalmist. But we don't avoid, ignore or devalue our pain or yours. We believe God meets us where we are. We don't believe you have to get it together before God will run into your life. It is actually in the midst of pain and brokenness that God does His greatest work.

We have big hopes. We believe that this project, to create content that invites people to collide with Jesus, has the potential to change your life and your friends' lives and your neighbors and on and on. We believe this because when people collide with Jesus they are never the same. We see this all the time in our ministry. When people run into who God is, they become who they are made to be. We have big God sized dreams that when we together, collide with Jesus, we will be changed and then we together can change the world.

How to use this study

We hand crafted this study for women just like you. It has been designed to be used in the way that works best, personally, for wherever you find yourself. We know that women experience a variety of different roles, seasons, and circumstances. We encourage you to engage this study with your morning cup o' coffee or pull it out of your handbag while you wait for your kids to be done with soccer practice. Grab it off the shelf when you are struggling to find purpose or invite some friends over and do it together. Jesus meets you along the way, so as you journey, doing whatever it is you do, may you enjoy colliding with Him.

We fashioned this study with freedom and joy in mind. Our hope is that colliding with Jesus brings gratification and not guilt, life and not condemnation, power and not oppression. So please be a friend to yourself and enter into this study with freedom knowing God invites you to come and collide with Him, not so He can critique you or grade you, but so He can love and spend time with you. God doesn't have an expectation of the number of pages you must read or a timeline of how fast you must complete this study. God won't be mad at you if you leave some reflection questions blank or even if you think a question we ask is dumb. It probably is. God merely wants to be with you. Enjoy your time with Him.

We constructed this study with a few simple prompts to invite your engagement.

Read

We will invite you to read a passage of Scripture that unfolds a collision with Jesus and corresponding Scripture that applies. Our desire is that as you see Jesus collide with others, you will also experience this living God collide with you.

Reflect

Our hope is that you would not just read or "know facts" about the Bible, but instead that you would allow your heart and mind to go to the deeper places: to reflect, to think, to mull, to consider. It is in our reflection that God can have some of His greatest conversations with each one of us. And it is in these conversations that transformation, guidance, wisdom and healing take place. We have intentionally written questions that will invite you to purposely reflect so that you can experience just that.

Ruminate

There will be points where we will encourage you to stop and chew, wrestle, learn or meditate on more. This is where ruminating on thoughts, Scripture, and quotes will bless you and invite you further into a collision with Jesus.

Respond

You can't stay the same and go with God. Every time Jesus collides with people they are forever transformed. He often calls us to take action, to pray, to move, to serve, to give, to lay down, to surrender, to not merely be "hearers" of the word but "doers". Our hope is that we will not just "study" God, but that we will become people who respond to our collisions with Jesus in a way that helps us see transformation in our own lives, that then leads to transformation in the lives of those around us.

Let's collide...

NOT ME.

1

YES, YOU.

WHAT IF GOD COULD
USE EXACTLY WHAT
WE'VE GOT TO PULL
OFF SOMETHING BIG?

I OFTEN SAY,
"not me"
AND MAYBE YOU DO TOO.

I will never forget the week I became a Christian. That was a huge deal for an irreligious girl who wanted nothing to do with Jesus and His people, a girl who never went to church and made fun of Christians, who wasn't sure there was a Creator, let alone a Savior, who had a lot of pain and blamed it all on God. But God chased me down and one day I handed my life over to Jesus. I remember literally extending my hands out and handing Him my pain, my past, my fears, my plans, and my dreams. (I'll save that story for another day…)

A week later, two guys came through my line at the grocery store, where I worked as a checker to afford my party life in college. They were buying massive amounts of baby food. It turned out they were youth leaders at the church I had randomly, or should I say divinely, walked into the week before and given my life to Christ. Of course, these youth leaders were playing some obnoxious game with whirled peas and carrots that was going to explain the Trinity or something. They eagerly invited me to come be a youth leader. I thought to myself, there is no way! NOT ME.

I had never been a part of a youth group, let alone qualified to lead at one. I wouldn't have a clue how to make a 15-year-old play with baby food and turn that into a bestie friendship with Jesus. I thought, "I am not even tight with God. I am a slut and I really like to drink peach schnapps and dance to Bob Marley." I mean how could God use a girl like me with lots o' baggage, abandonment issues, a load of insecurities, little knowledge of Jesus and no church background? What a wounded mess. I didn't fit the profile. But these two men were convincing so I showed up at a rowdy youth group for the first time… as a leader.

I often felt insecure to help people for God. I was sure I didn't belong and I wasn't good enough to be a "leader". But the more I showed up to help the kids, the more Jesus started helping me. Crazy things started happening. I was waking up in the middle of the night with words coming out of my mouth and stories that I had to write down because I couldn't wait to share them with struggling high schoolers.

11

I met with the youth pastor and his wife to ask what they thought was happening to me. They said, "We believe God is calling you into vocational ministry."

"What's vocational ministry?!" I honestly had no idea.

They answered, "It's when ministry is your calling and your career."

Stomping my feet on the inside, I said "Nooooooooooooooo!" NOT ME.

I was pursuing a business degree at Western Washington University so I could be a leader in the corporate world, make the big bucks and be a boss. I was planning on marrying the pilot I had been dating for years and I was going to bring Jesus with me. He was my new friend and He could come along. I wasn't a Jesus follower, I was a Jesus dragger. One day after class, I was walking on a trail above campus and words came out of my mouth. It was my voice, but God's words. He said "I want to use your life to proclaim my power. Sure, you believe in me but I want more than that for you and from you. When you get off this trail, you choose, are you gonna go your own way or follow me?" I wanted to scream NOT ME but when I stepped off that trail I knew where I was going…

I applied to be a pastoral intern at my church. I was sure they would find out who I really was and turn me down lickety split. On my third interview, I sat across from the senior pastor and he asked me if I was willing to try preaching. I said "Me? No way! Never! I will clean toilets, greet old women, play dodgeball and talk to sassy teenagers about Jesus, but I will NEVER speak up front and actually have something to say that will change lives. I have never taken Bible 101 or a speech class, plus people will see my booty and no one needs to see that. NOT ME."

They turned me down for the internship. "Of course, they did," I thought. "I could never preach." I had an opportunity to be used by God to do amazing things but I walked away because I didn't believe God could use me…

Reflect

How do you walk away from opportunities to do amazing things because you struggle to believe God can use you?

What things do you believe about yourself that cause you to do this?

How often do you say, NOT ME? I have a feeling it's all too often. I sit across from you guys. I go to parties with you. I stand on the sports sidelines with you. I have way too much coffee in the same coffee shops you do. I hear the disappointment some of you feel about your calling. I hear the self-debasing statements you utter - the ones that hinder and harm, rather than unleash and inspire. I hear the excuses that keep your dreams stifled - I make them too. But I also hear your passion. I hear your prayers to be purposed. I hear your heart that desires to make your life truly count. And yet you keep saying, NOT ME.

This NOT ME mantra is what has us saying no to opportunities that God has for us all the time. This NOT ME has us dreaming small instead of big. This NOT ME has us discouraged and disappointed. It has us cowering in fear at the thought of risking and saying yes to God and God-sized appointments. This NOT ME has us envying other

THIS "not me" MANTRA IS WHAT HAS US SAYING, "NO" TO OPPORTUNITIES GOD HAS FOR US.

13

women, wishing we could be like them because we think maybe if we were like "her", we would feel purposed. This NOT ME has us living in the past, dreaming of a future that our present makes no space to find. This NOT ME has us reading every self-help book we can get our hands on only to finish each one, still as lost as we started. This NOT ME mantra makes our God small and our faith smaller.

This NOT ME is doing nothing for the people all around us crying out for help and rescue. This NOT ME doesn't feed the hungry. This NOT ME doesn't clothe those with no clothes. This NOT ME doesn't speak up for those who can't speak up for themselves. This NOT ME doesn't walk alongside struggling teenagers in need of our presence. This NOT ME doesn't stand up against bullies. This NOT ME doesn't house people with no place to call home. This NOT ME doesn't preach good news to people desperate for it. This NOT ME doesn't bring healing to those who are wounded. No, this NOT ME keeps us small, God smaller and the impact we can have on a hurting world inconsequential.

Reflect

YOUR **"not me"** MANTRA HAS YOU....

(check all the boxes that apply)

○ Dreaming small

○ Discouraged and disappointed

○ Afraid to take risks

○ Envying other women

○ Living in the past

○ Reading self-help books with no transformation

○ Making God small and faith smaller

○ Lacking compassion for hurting people

This NOT ME has some of you waiting. You are waiting to get cooler. You are waiting for a degree. You are waiting for this season to pass. You are waiting to get tighter with the Big Man upstairs. You are waiting to sound more spiritual. You are waiting to be like Suzy. Some of you are waiting for your personality and talents to change. You are waiting for your insecurities to be replaced with a strong self-confidence. And you can wait 'til you're blue in the face honey, 'cause you being more isn't what's gonna pull off amazing things in your life.

Reflect

How do you feel like the world around you is bombarding you to be more than you already are?

When I walked away from the opportunity to be a pastoral intern and do something only God could do through me, I kept thinking about this Jesus I had recently begun colliding with. Jesus fiercely challenges our confidence problem. Everything I saw in Him, even as a new believer, told me that my NOT ME was false. I was believing lies. I was letting my past determine my present. I was letting my wounds win and my insecurities call me. Are you doing that?

Reflect

What lies are you believing about yourself?

YOU *being more* IS NOT WHAT IS GOING TO PULL OFF AMAZING THINGS IN YOUR LIFE.

How are you letting your past determine your present?

How are you letting your wounds win in your life?

How are you letting your insecurities determine what you are called to do?'

Decades ago, Jesus' very presense challenged my confidence problem and has continued to ever since. Everything I saw in Him made everything in me turn around. So I went back to the Senior Pastor and said, "God told me, 'Never say no to what I can do through you.' So here I am taking Him at His word that He can use even me." And that was when the pastor graciously handed me back the opportunity to do the internship. The day I stopped saying NOT ME to myself, but instead said YES YOU to God was the day I became an intern at a church for God's sake.

Reflect

Imagine if your past, your insecurities, and your wounds no longer held you back. What do you picture your life looking like when you stop letting the NOT ME's get in the way?

Ruminate

Now to him who is able to do immeasurably more than all we ask or imagine, according to his power that is at work within us **Ephesians 3:20**

Respond

Pray to the One who is able to do immeasurably more than all we can ask or imagine.

Lord,

I have let my brokenness and insecurities drown out your call for my life. I often doubt that you can use me to do amazing things. Please help me to stop living out my Not Me's. Give me faith to believe that You, God can do amazing things through my life. Give me faith to allow You to enter my past experiences, my insecurities, and my wounds. I want to trust you to heal me, change me and use my life for great things. Lord please run into my life in the place I am right now and meet me here. Amen.

We want to invite you throughout this Bible Study to collide with the One who wants to meet you in your

not me's

and turn them into

yes, you's

During our time together, we will follow this Jesus as He uses a li'l boy and his measly lunch to do amazing things. As you watch Jesus collide with this boy, He too will collide with you.

A NEW MANTRA

YES, YOU.

WHAT IF GOD COULD
USE EXACTLY WHAT
WE'VE GOT TO PULL
OFF SOMETHING BIG?

20

Read

Some time after this, Jesus crossed to the far shore of the Sea of Galilee (that is, the Sea of Tiberias), ² and a great crowd of people followed him because they saw the signs he had performed by healing the sick. ³ Then Jesus went up on a mountainside and sat down with his disciples. ⁴ The Jewish Passover Festival was near. ⁵ When Jesus looked up and saw a great crowd coming toward him, he said to Philip, "Where shall we buy bread for these people to eat?"⁶ He asked this only to test him, for he already had in mind what he was going to do. ⁷ Philip answered him, "It would take more than half a year's wages to buy enough bread for each one to have a bite!"⁸ Another of his disciples, Andrew, Simon Peter's brother, spoke up, ⁹ "Here is a boy with five small barley loaves and two small fish, but how far will they go among so many?" ¹⁰ Jesus said, "Have the people sit down." There was plenty of grass in that place, and they sat down (about five thousand men were there). ¹¹ Jesus then took the loaves, gave thanks, and distributed to those who were seated as much as they wanted. He did the same with the fish. ¹² When they had all had enough to eat, he said to his disciples, "Gather the pieces that are left over. Let nothing be wasted." ¹³ So they gathered them and filled twelve baskets with the pieces of the five barley loaves left over by those who had eaten. ¹⁴ After the people saw the sign Jesus performed, they began to say, "Surely this is the Prophet who is to come into the world." ¹⁵ Jesus, knowing that they intended to come and make him king by force, withdrew again to a mountain by himself.
John 6:1-15

In John 6, the collision we are centering around, there is a boy who must have thought, NOT ME. According to commentator E.A. Blum, this story is apparently the only miracle recorded in all four gospels (except for Jesus' resurrection),[1] which shows us this must be a pretty important collision. It starts out with a huge crowd of people following Jesus because He was healing the sick. You know, sometimes I think we read the Bible like we read CNN News - Like "thousands of people were displaced from their homes", like "six people were shot at a mall," like "another middle schooler committed suicide".

When the Bible says *"a great crowd of people followed him because they saw the signs he had performed by healing the sick"...* **John 6:2**, these were people's mothers with cancer; these were people's brothers with mental illness; these were people's children with epilepsy and Jesus was healing them.

---

[1] Blum, E.A. (1985). John. In J.F. Walvoord & R.B. Zuck (eds.), The Bible Knowledge Commentary: An Exposition of the Scriptures (Vol. 2, p.293). Wheaton, IL: Victor Books

Ruminate

This collision can also be found in:

Matthew 14:13-21, Mark 6:30-44, Luke 9:10-17

I would follow Him too.

I would get a fanny pack,

throw some sunscreen

and some Trail mix

in that puppy and I would

trek with Jesus

to Timbuktu because He has the

power to heal someone I love.

22

Reflect

Imagine someone you love who needs healing.

Write their name here:

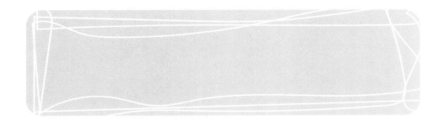

If you lived in this time and place and you knew there was a man named Jesus who had the power to heal the person you know needs healing, what lengths would you go to access or follow Him?

On this particular day, on a mountainside, Jesus saw a great crowd coming toward him. Can you imagine the pressures He felt? Can you imagine the demands that pressed in on Jesus, the despair that begged of Him and the sad stories thrown at Him? Here they came, thousands of them. I think Jesus' response is funny. He could have supernaturally vanished, like abracadabra, poof, Jesus is at an Irish pub listening to bagpipers. He could have had his disciples put on a show - you know, some kind of cheesy Christian theatrical play with

live sheep and goats. He could have asked the people to break up in groups and share their happys and crappys. But He doesn't. Instead, He says to Philip, *"Where shall we buy bread for these people to eat?"* **John 6:5**

When I read this passage I think, "Why does Jesus insist on feeding them? Can't they go home and have nachos later?" The Bible says, Jesus *"asked this only to test him."* **John 6:6**

Reflect

How do you feel about a God who wants to test us?

In your opinion, what was the test Jesus was giving Philip?

We don't like to think about a God who might test us, but Jesus' question was to help Philip realize what Jesus already knew. The Bible says, *"for he already had in mind what he was going to do."* **John 6:6**

 are we in a scenario where we freak out thinking, "There is no way!" Meanwhile, God is sitting there confident in His plan. Maybe this can be our new mantra: **God already has in mind what He is going to do.**

mantra

noun | man.tra | 'mantre/
a statement or slogan repeated frequently

Maybe, when our kids come home from middle school lost and hurting and we have no control over making it better, we can say "God already has in mind what He is going to do." Maybe when the love of our life decides we aren't good enough, and we go to bed alone in our grief, we can remind ourselves "God already has in mind what He is going to do." Maybe when we are faced with an opportunity to do something amazing and we see absolutely no way it's possible, we can say to ourselves: "Self, you have a God who already has in mind what He is going to do."

Reflect

How would it change your mindset if you stood confidently on this belief in your current circumstances?

How often do you say things in your head, repeating a negative mantra that creates fear, anxiety or panic? How often do you say things like:

- ○ I'm just average.
- ○ I'm too busy.
- ○ My life is a mess.
- ○ I'm not like so and so.
- ○ I'm not spiritual enough.
- ○ Other

In the first column, write down some of the circumstances you are dealing with right now which seem impossible. In the column on the right, practice your new mantra, "God already has in mind what He is going to do".

Things that feel impossible	God already has in mind what He is going to do
a relationship of mine that feels broken	God already has in mind what He is going to do

Respond

What are some specific actions you can take this week to replace your negative mantras with your new mantra, "God already has in mind what He is going to do."? List these and then pray that God will give you the strength to live them out.

INFERIOR OFFERINGS

YES, YOU.

WHAT IF GOD COULD
USE EXACTLY WHAT
WE'VE GOT TO PULL
OFF SOMETHING BIG?

Read

⁷ Philip answered him, "It would take more than half a year's wages to buy enough bread for each one to have a bite!" ⁸ Another of his disciples, Andrew, Simon Peter's brother, spoke up,⁹ "Here is a boy with five small barley loaves and two small fish, but how far will they go among so many?" **John 6: 7-9**

In this collision, Philip answered Jesus the way I think we would: *"It would take more than half a year's wages to buy enough bread for each one to have a bite!"* **John 6:7**

Philip is probably looking at Jesus thinking we will feed these people when pigs fly, when hell freezes over, when Satan ice skates to work. How will we ever feed five thousand people on the side of this mountain, on the fly, with no plan, no caterer, and no money? "Oh Jesus and his pipe dreams", Philip is probably uttering under his breath.

Reflect

What is another way to phrase what Philip is getting at?

If you were Philip, what would you have suggested?

Another of his disciples, Andrew, Simon Peter's brother, spoke up,

"HERE IS A BOY WITH FIVE SMALL BARLEY LOAVES AND TWO SMALL FISH, BUT *how far will they go* AMONG SO MANY?" **John 6:9**

Imagine this li'l boy is following the crowd. Who knows, maybe he was intrigued by Jesus. Maybe he was drug along by his mama who needed a miracle. Maybe he was wondering what all the hullabaloo was about. Regardless of why this boy happened to find himself on the same hillside as Jesus, I am almost 100% sure he didn't think he would be called out nor did he most likely want to be.

There he was with his li'l lunch, an inferior lunch, no less. Barley bread was cheap. It was the bread of the poor. One commentator said barley was called the "food of beasts" and "an offering for a woman who has committed adultery." [1] Here this poor kid was packing poor man bread and a few sardines in his lunch. Getting called out would highlight just how inferior he felt and most likely he didn't want to give up his lunch- it was after all, what he had to eat.

Reflect

Put your catering hat on. How many people could you feed with five small barley loaves and two small fish?

[1]Barclay, W. (Ed.). (1975). The Gospel of John (Vol. 1, pp. 202–203). Philadelphia, PA: The Westminster John Knox Press.

If two sardines and five loaves of Wonder bread was all you had to serve your guests, what would you do?

○   Cancel the event.

○   Order Domino's.

○   Give everyone a lecture about starving people in other parts of the world.

○   Convince everyone it is a good time to fast and pray.

○   Move things along so everyone could leave.

○   Apologize profusely for not being a good host.

○   Other _____.

What do you think this boy is thinking when Andrew calls him out in verse 9?

What picture does this paint of the little boy's life that his lunch consisted of "food of the beasts" and the type of bread an "adulterous woman" would use as an offering?

This boy had an inferior type of bread. In what ways does that resonate with you and what you feel you have to offer?

Ruminate

Read the following Scriptures to encourage you in the places you feel inferior:

- *²⁹ He gives strength to the weary and increases the power of the weak. ³⁰ Even youths grow tired and weary, and young men stumble and fall; ³¹ but those who hope in the LORD will renew their strength. They will soar on wings like eagles; they will run and not grow weary, they will walk and not be faint.* **Isaiah 40:29-31**

- *In the same way the Spirit also helps our weakness; for we do not know how to pray as we should, but the Spirit Himself intercedes for us with groanings too deep for words.* **Romans 8:26 NASB**

- *²⁷ But God chose the foolish things of the world to shame the wise; God chose the weak things of the world to shame the strong.²⁸ God chose the lowly things of this world and despised things - and the things that are not- to nullify the things that are,²⁹ so that no one may boast before him.* **1 Corinthians 1:27-29**

- *⁹ But he said to me, "My grace is sufficient for you, for my power is made perfect in weakness." Therefore I will boast all the more gladly about my weaknesses, so that Christ's power may rest on me. ¹⁰ That is why, for Christ's sake, I delight in weaknesses, in insults, in hardships, in persecutions, in difficulties. For when I am weak, then I am strong.* **2 Corinthians 12:9-10**

- *There is neither Jew nor Greek, there is neither slave nor free, there is no male and female, for you are all one in Christ Jesus.* **Galatians 3:28 ESV**

Reflect

Which of these Scriptures did you need to hear today? Re-write it in the space below as you claim it to be true for your own life.

Respond

Take some time to write from your heart:

God, I feel inferior in these ways...

But I know You are superior in these ways...

BEING AN ANDREW

YES, YOU.

WHAT IF GOD COULD
USE EXACTLY WHAT
WE'VE GOT TO PULL
OFF SOMETHING BIG?

Read

⁵ When Jesus looked up and saw a great crowd coming toward him, he said to Philip, "Where shall we buy bread for these people to eat?" ⁶ He asked this only to test him, for he already had in mind what he was going to do.⁷ Philip answered him, "It would take more than half a year's wages to buy enough bread for each one to have a bite!" ⁸ Another of his disciples, Andrew, Simon Peter's brother, spoke up,⁹ "Here is a boy with five small barley loaves and two small fish, but how far will they go among so many?" **John 6:5-9**

Out of 5,000 people, Andrew calls out the potential in this one boy and his loser lunch. Oh, how we need Andrews in our lives and oh, how we need to be Andrews.

> ## potential
> *adjective* | po.ten.tial | pe'ten(t)SHel
> *latent qualities or abilities that may be developed
> and lead to future success or usefulness*

Seeing potential in someone requires perceiving something that may be developed but hasn't yet been. There is an element of faith in seeing potential in people. When you see potential in another person, it often requires looking past obstacles, what currently "is", present status, inabilities, weaknesses and failures. Seeing potential in someone requires you looking at someone and moving past your view of them that says: "there is no way". Seeing potential in people requires you to move past your doubts and graciously, like Andrew, still call out the possibility in another. Seeing potential in people requires trusting God for what He can do in another person's life.

Reflect

What did Andrew see that this little boy had?

What did Andrew believe God could do with that?

$\mathcal{I}$ $will$ never forget the youth pastor who threw me in to speak for the first time to nearly a hundred kids. I had to get up and have something to say about God and I was gonna have to say it in a way that would connect with sassy teenagers. I had never been to youth group. I was a new believer. There wasn't anything in me that thought this was a good idea!

This youth pastor saw something in me that I did not see in myself. He believed God could do something through me that I did not believe. Sure, he could have had a long list of doubts about me, my past, my choices, my spiritual maturity, and could have questioned my ability to be used by God. But it was this "Andrew" who instead of doubting saw great promise. It was this man seeing the potential in me that changed the trajectory of my life. It was his encouragement, prodding, and voice that pushed me to lean into who I was becoming rather than stay stuck as who I had been. Who knew that God would end up calling me to use my voice to be His messenger as my life's work? What a gift to have people who believe for us what do we don't believe for ourselves. What a gift to have people on the journey who inspire our potential!

Reflect

Do you currently have an Andrew in your life, someone who calls out your potential to be used by God?

If so, what does that person see in you that you have trouble seeing in yourself?

If not, what are some things you can do to seek out a person for your life who will encourage your potential?

We often spend time seeing people for who they have been or currently are. We see their flaws and their failures. We see they are chronically late, irresponsible or lack a filter. We begin to put people in boxes thinking things like: "What a flake, she's off, he's a stoner, they are so immature".

What if we became the ultimate potential spotters like Jesus is? Jesus saw people for who they were meant to become. What if we saw the good in people and called it out? What if we believed with all of our hearts that God could change anyone and we inspired that change? What if instead of seeing failure, we saw the power of grace? What if instead of seeing faults, we saw the might of God's power in and through a life? Spotting what could be in our kids, our spouses, our friends and our enemies, might possibly be a world changing trait that we have the ability to live out with endless supply.

Reflect

Why is it sometimes hard for you to see people for who they could be rather than who they already are?

What does seeing potential in someone require you to believe that God can do in and through them?

How can you start seeing the potential in people that God sees in them?

Ruminate

God is the ultimate potential spotter. God sees in us who we do not see in ourselves. God saw the Peter in Simon, who Simon did not see in himself. God saw the woman who would be used to change her village, in the get around girl at the well. God saw the man in his right mind, in the demon possessed cutter in the tombs. God saw the preacher, Paul, in the Christian killer, Saul. May we have eyes to see others like God does.

Fill in the missing parts of this table with other examples from Scripture where God called out the potential in someone who needed encouragement.

Person who needed encouragement	Scripture	Potential God saw in them
Sarah	Genesis 18:10-15	God saw the mother in her she did not see herself
	Luke 5:1-11	
Mary	Luke 1:26-38	
	Judges 6:11-14	God saw a mighty warrior in a hiding wimp
	Matthew 9:9-13	

Reflect

How does it encourage you that God sees in you the potential that you don't see in yourself?

BUT ENCOURAGE ONE ANOTHER DAILY, AS LONG AS IT IS CALLED "*Today,*" SO THAT NONE OF YOU MAY BE HARDENED BY SIN'S DECEITFULNESS. HEBREWS 3:13

How do you need to lean into God's belief in the great potential that your life is capable of?

Think of someone you spot great potential in and write their name here:

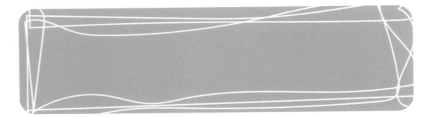

What are some of the specific things you see in that person?

What do you believe God could do in and through them?

Hebrew 3:13 says, *"But encourage one another daily, as long as it is called "today," so that none of you may be hardened by sin's deceiftfulness."* This is what some call "one another" verse. What can you do to encourage the one in whom you see potential?

(For more inspiring "one anothers," see pages 47-48)

encourage

verb | en.cour.age | /in'kerij
give support, confidence, or hope to someone

Ruminate

Look up these scriptures about encouragement. Write them in the space provided and circle the one you most resonate with.

- 1 Thessalonians 5:11

- Hebrews 10:24-25

- Romans 15:5

Respond

We are called to encourage one another as long as today is called today. And I am pretty sure today is not called yesterday, nor tomorrow. Write a prayer asking God to help you encourage someone who needs encouragement. Pray for the person whose name you wrote down and ask God to become in them who He has made them to be. Pray for your heart to see potential in those you often struggle to see potential in, remembering that God can use us spotting potential in another to change countless lives! Just think about how many lives were impacted by Andrew calling out the potential in one unlikely little boy and his measly lunch!

One Anothers of the New Testament

Be at peace with each other **Mark 9:50**

Wash one another's feet John **13:14**

Love one another as I have loved you **John 13:34**

Love one another **John 13:35**

Love each other as I have loved you **John 15:12**

Love each other **John 15:17**

Be devoted to one another in love **Romans 12:10**

Honor one another above yourselves **Romans 12:10**

Live in harmony with one another **Romans 12:16**

Let no debt remain outstanding, except the continuing debt to love one another **Romans 13:8**

Let us stop passing judgment on one another **Romans 14:13**

Accept one another, then, just as Christ accepted you **Romans 15:7**

Instruct one another **Romans 15:14**

Greet one another with a holy kiss **Romans 16:16, 1 Corinthians 16:20, 2 Corinthians 13:12**

Have equal concern for each other **I Corinthians 12:25**

Serve one another humbly in love **Galatians 5:13**

If you bite and devour each other, watch out or you will be destroyed by each other **Galatians 5:15**

Let us not become conceited, provoking and envying each other **Galatians 5:26**

Carry each other's burdens **Galatians 6:2**

Be completely humble and gentle; be patient, bearing with one another in love **Ephesians 4:2**

Be kind and compassionate to one another, forgiving each other, just as in Christ God forgave you **Ephesians 4:32**

Speak to one another with psalms, hymns and songs from the Spirit **Ephesians 5:19**

Submit to one another out of reverence for Christ **Ephesians 5:21**

In humility value others above yourselves **Philippians 2:3**

Do not lie to each other **Colossians 3:9**

Bear with each other and forgive one another if any of you has a grievance against someone **Colossians 3:13**

Teach and admonish one another with all wisdom through psalms, hymns, and songs from the Spirit **Colossians 3:16**

Love each other **I Thessalonians 4:9**

Encourage one another **I Thessalonians 4:18**

Build each other up **I Thessalonians 5:11**

Encourage one another daily **Hebrews 3:13**

Spur one another on toward love and good deeds **Hebrews 10:24**

Encourage one another **Hebrews 10:25**

Do not slander one another **James 4:11**

Don't grumble against one another **James 5:9**

Confess your sins to each other and pray for each other **James 5:16**

Love one another deeply, from the heart **1 Peter 1:22**

Love one another, be compassionate and humble **I Peter 3:8**

Love each other deeply, because love covers a multitude of sins **I Peter 4:8**

Offer hospitality to one another without grumbling **I Peter 4:9**

Clothe yourselves with humility toward one another **I Peter 5:5**

Greet one another with a kiss of love **I Peter 5:14**

Love one another **I John 3:11**

Love one another as He commanded us **1 John 3:23**

Love one another, for love comes from God **1 John 4:7**

Love one another **1 John 4:11**

Love one another **2 John 5**

Found on wecollide.net/resources

HUNGRY

5

YES, YOU.

WHAT IF GOD COULD
USE EXACTLY WHAT
WE'VE GOT TO PULL
OFF SOMETHING BIG?

Read

10 Jesus said, "Have the people sit down." There was plenty of grass in that place, and they sat down (about five thousand men were there). 11 Jesus then took the loaves, gave thanks, and distributed to those who were seated as much as they wanted. He did the same with the fish.
John 6:10-11

 that many people to sit seems like a modern day miracle. This scene sounds so much like the Shepherd whom the Psalmist refers to in **Psalm 23:2,** *"He makes me lie down in green pastures; he leads me beside quiet waters."* The parallel story found in **Mark 6:34** says, *"When Jesus landed and saw a large crowd, he had compassion on them because they were like sheep without a shepherd; so he began teaching them many things."* Jesus feeding these people on the hillside was Jesus caring for his sheep and like a good Shepherd, He wanted for them rest and food. The crowd sat down in the grass and Jesus then took the loaves and gave thanks…

Reflect

Have you heard of Jesus taking bread and giving thanks elsewhere?

Was it necessary to feed the people that day?

What does Jesus providing one meal to these people reveal about Him?

51

This Shepherd, He knew what He was going to do, both here on this mountain side in this miracle, but also one day coming soon. We do see later, in **Luke 22:19**: Jesus ALSO *took bread, gave thanks and broke it. He gave it to them* (the disciples), *saying, "This is my body given for you; do this in remembrance of me."* This Shepherd knew the day on the hillside with the 5,000 people, that in the same way He broke bread and gave thanks to feed them, He too would be broken and give thanks to save them. We end up seeing later that Jesus would be broken as bread in **Matthew 27**, *"27 Then the governor's soldiers took Jesus into the Praetorium and gathered the whole company of soldiers around him. 28 They stripped him and put a scarlet robe on him, 29 and then twisted together a crown of thorns and set it on his head. They put a staff in his right hand. Then they knelt in front of him and mocked him. "Hail, king of the Jews!" they said. 30 They spit on him, and took the staff and struck him on the head again and again. 31 After they had mocked him, they took off the robe and put his own clothes on him. Then they led him away to crucify him."*

Ruminate

Read the following passages and underline what Christ being broken accomplishes for us.

- *But God demonstrates his own love for us in this: While we were still sinners, Christ died for us.* **Romans 5:8**

- *For Christ also suffered once for sins, the righteous for the unrighteous, to bring you to God. He was put to death in the body but made alive in the Spirit.* **1 Peter 3:18**

- *He died for us so that, whether we are awake or asleep, we may live together with him.* **1 Thessalonians 5:10**

- *For if, while we were God's enemies, we were reconciled to him through the death of his Son, how much more, having been reconciled, shall we be saved through his life!* **Romans 5:10**

Jesus' body broken for us accomplished showing us the fullness of God's love, reconciled our broken relationship with God and guaranteed we will live together with Him, both now and forever. Christ being broken was to come sometime after this collision with Jesus and the 5,000. For now He broke bread, gave thanks and distributed to those who were seated as much as they wanted. He did the same with the fish. This was crazy! Jesus took one kid's sack lunch and fed thousands! But Jesus gave away more than bread...

Read the following passages and underline what Jesus generously gave.

- *23For I received from the Lord what I also passed on to you: The Lord Jesus, on the night he was betrayed, took bread, 24and when he had given thanks, he broke it and said, "This is my body, which is for you; do this in remembrance of me." 25In the same way, after supper he took the cup, saying, "This cup is the new covenant in my blood; do this, whenever you drink it, in remembrance of me." 26For whenever you eat this bread and drink this cup, you proclaim the Lord's death until he comes.* **1 Corinthians 11:23-26**

- *...Walk in the way of love, just as Christ loved us and gave himself up for us as a fragrant offering and sacrifice to God.* **Ephesians 5:2**

- *[13]While we wait for the blessed hope—the appearing of the glory of our great God and Savior, Jesus Christ, [14]who gave himself for us to redeem us from all wickedness and to purify for himself a people that are his very own, eager to do what is good.* **Titus 2:13-14**

- *I am the living bread that came down from heaven. Whoever eats this bread will live forever. This bread is my flesh, which I will give for the life of the world."* **John 6:51**

Jesus would end up giving away more than bread, but His very Self for all those who are hungry. He knew that all the bread in the world wouldn't satisfy our appetite. He knew that the most bountiful meal wouldn't fill us. It is in fact our appetite that often leads to our hunger. Jesus referred to Himself as the bread of life because He offers Himself as the only meal that we will ever partake in that will satisfy, fill and nourish. How cool is it that we have a God who runs into our lives and wants to feed us in a very practical way, with loaves and fish, but also in a deeply spiritual way by giving away Himself, broken as bread, and ours for the taking.

Reflect

How are you hungry?

How do you need more than bread?

FARMERS EVERY-
WHERE PROVIDE
BREAD FOR ALL
HUMANITY, BUT IT
IS CHRIST ALONE
WHO IS THE BREAD
OF LIFE...EVEN IF
ALL THE PHYSICAL
HUNGER OF THE
WORLD WAS SATIS-
FIED, EVEN IF
EVERYONE WHO IS
HUNGRY WERE
SATISFIED, EVEN IF
EVERYONE WHO IS
HUNGRY WERE FED
BY HIS OR HER OWN
LABOR OR BY THE
GENEROSITY OF
OTHERS, THE DEEP-
EST HUNGER OF MAN
WOULD STILL
EXIST...THEREFORE,
I SAY, COME, ALL
OF YOU, TO CHRIST.
POPE JOHN PAUL II

How does it make you feel to know that this same Jesus, who out of His great compassion unnecessarily fed all of these people, would later perform the necessary miracle of giving His very body for YOU, so you would no longer be hungry?

Jesus promises to be all that we need to fulfill our hunger. How can you partake in Him when you have "hunger pains"?

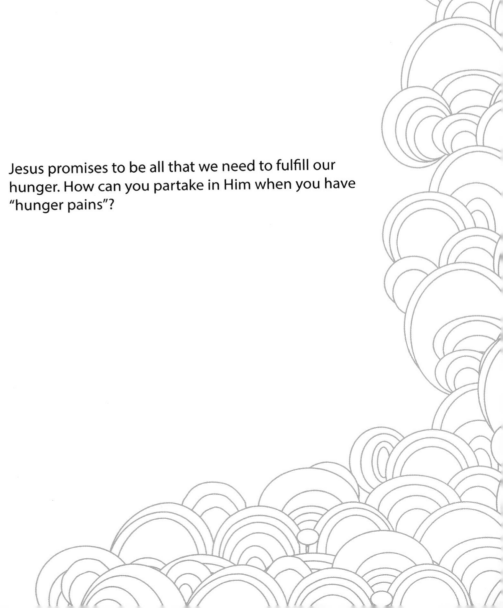

Respond

As we can see, Jesus is a God who gives us Himself. When someone gives you something, you respond. Make space here to acknowledge God's gift to you, of Himself.

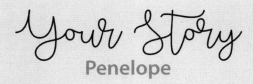
Penelope

We encourage women to bravely and authentically tell their stories as they really are. We hope this "your story" meets you in yours...

It was a regular rainy November morning when Penelope, a first grader in my classroom, passed me a handwritten note asking for donations to her food pantry. The note asked school families to drop off food in the hallway to be distributed during the upcoming holiday season. I assumed she was talking about giving it to the local food bank. I couldn't have been more mistaken! As the next couple of weeks went by, brown grocery bags were left outside my classroom door for Penelope to take home. After getting more information, I realized Penelope wasn't offering the food to the food bank but to her neighbors.

Penelope and her dad had taken an old entertainment center, made some structural changes, painted it, and set it in her front yard where a mailbox might be found. If one opened the door to this rebuilt creation, shelves full of food and random household items would be seen. A sign placed above the top shelf read:

> ### Community Pantry
> *Take something*
> *Leave something*
> *For families in need*

The contents of the pantry emptied quickly and constantly needed replenishing. Hence, Penelope's notes asking her classmates for donations.

Months went by, and I didn't give it another thought. Until March. As a member of the Collide ministry team, I sat in an event planning meeting where we were brainstorming ideas to try and illustrate this story where Jesus changed the lunch offered by a small boy into a feast enjoyed by thousands of hungry people. We hashed over ideas that would somehow allow women to see that their gifts, however small, could be used by God in big ways. The message we were trying to convey at this particular event was, "Yes, you!" If a little kid could offer his measly lunch that resulted in God doing big things, then so could we. Even though ideas filled an entire whiteboard, the team was stuck. We couldn't figure out how to make this concept of "Yes, you" come alive--until Penelope's Pantry was revisited.

A big surprise awaited the sweet, freckle-faced, heart-bigger-than-gold, seven-year old Penelope. Those coming to the event were urged to bring food from home. Penelope's mom was happily on board with the idea and suggested we ask for donations centered around sack lunch food. Summer was coming and children in her neighborhood would need lunches.

Penelope was asked to share on stage, in front of hundreds of women, about her pantry. She bravely answered questions and showed some slides depicting the building process. The audience "awwwwed" and clapped as Penelope left the stage. She then promptly left with her mom to enjoy an ice cream treat somewhere in town. Little did she know that in her absence, women would be urged to pull out their phones and text their friends and families to ask them to bring even more food to the location of this Collide event. Local residents came in droves to drop off food for her pantry. A line of cars went around the block as the Collide team ran out to collect it. Sack after sack of food was lugged to the front of the stage. It was a sight to see!

As the event came to a close, Penelope returned and was ushered in through the back door, thinking we were just going to share some more about her pantry. When the time came, I blindfolded her and told her we had a big surprise for her. As I walked her back out onto the stage, she giggled and pulled her gramma's shawl snuggly around her shoulders. The blindfold came off. Penelope's eyes grew big as she realized the mounds and pounds of food on stage were for her pantry. She smiled and said, "Me likey!" The women laughed, clapped and cried as she walked down the aisle to meet her mom. We held hands and tears rolled down her face. She bounded into her mother's arms, and through a muffled hug exclaimed, "Mom! There is so much food!"

It was a beautiful act of kindness all around, yet there was a big problem: as the team planned the event, we had no way of knowing how much food would come in—a few bags, a lot of bags? Well, not THIS much food! In the midst of planning the day, we failed to find a way to transport it! As we scrambled to figure it out, two young women approached me and asked if we needed help driving the food to Penelope's house. Out of the blue! Another small miracle. They buzzed to their respective homes and showed up with two large vans! The load was so huge, Penelope was able to share some of it with two other families in the community who were so inspired by her story, they decided to start their own neighborhood pantries.

God took this one sweet, little girl with a giant heart and used her to change lives. Not only is she taking care of some very basic needs, she is also encouraging me and others to say yes to God. If God can use a seven year old to do amazing things, surely, He can use me as well.

Written by Tamara Lindhout

WHAT'S IN YOUR LUNCHBOX?

YES, YOU.

WHAT IF GOD COULD
USE EXACTLY WHAT
WE'VE GOT TO PULL
OFF SOMETHING BIG?

Read

⁵ When Jesus looked up and saw a great crowd coming toward him, he said to Philip, "Where shall we buy bread for these people to eat?" ⁶ He asked this only to test him, for he already had in mind what he was going to do. ⁷ Philip answered him, "It would take more than half a year's wages to buy enough bread for each one to have a bite!" ⁸ Another of his disciples, Andrew, Simon Peter's brother, spoke up, ⁹ "Here is a boy with five small barley loaves and two small fish, but how far will they go among so many?" ¹⁰ Jesus said, "Have the people sit down." There was plenty of grass in that place, and they sat down (about five thousand men were there). ¹¹ Jesus then took the loaves, gave thanks, and distributed to those who were seated as much as they wanted. He did the same with the fish. **John 6:5-11**

What strikes me most about this collision is that Jesus used what this boy had. That's what He does. God uses what we have to do amazing things. Not what others have. Not what we wish we had. Not what we think we need, but what we already have. Our story. Our experiences. Our gifts. Our learning lessons. Our pain. Our resources.

GOD USES *what we have* TO DO AMAZING THINGS.

Reflect

What are you thinking you need to get, be or accomplish in order for God to use you to do amazing things?

Can you think of an example of someone you know who allowed God to take the little they had and use it to do something big?

What about their story inspires you?

We don't have to go out and get more degrees, or more talent or a new body. We don't need to get more money, a new career or a new personality. God doesn't need us to go out and get a better lunch. God can use what we already have to pull off something big. He does it all the time. Let's look at who and what God has used in history with humanity to pull off big things.

Person	What they had	The amazing thing God did	Scripture
David	Sling and a stone	Gave the Israelites victory over the Philistines.	1 Samuel 17
	Small jar of olive oil		2 Kings 4: 1-7
	Staff willing attitude Faith	Parted the Sea so the Israelites could cross on dry land.	
Rahab			Joshua 2 Joshua 6 Matthew 1:5 Hebrews 11:31 James 2:25
Simon Peter			Luke 5:1-11
		Forgiveness and healing.	Matthew 9:1-8 Mark 2:1-12 Luke 5:17-26
Paul			Acts 22:1-21

Reflect

What did this boy have that caused Andrew to call him out?

What do you have that God can use?

LET'S PROBE A LITTLE DEEPER INTO WHAT YOU HAVE THAT GOD CAN USE:

What gifts do you have?

What experiences do you have?

What resources do you have?

What pain have you experienced that God can use to help others in theirs?

What lessons have you learned that God can use?

What do people call out in you that you possess?

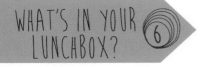
Calling all artists! It's time to break out your colored pencils and fill in this lunch box with "what you have"...

Now what do you have?

66

Respond

I think a lot of us are waiting to have something better, bigger, more successful, more put together or more impressive inside our "lunchbox". But God is not waiting for you to get something more. God can use what you have right now to do amazing things in this world. That's what God does. Take time to express to God how amazing it is that He is more than able to use exactly what you have to pull off something big.

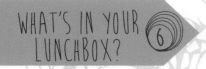

know this:

The moment you hand to God what you already have, is the moment God will begin writing amazing stories in your life. As it was for this boy, so it can be for you.

I'M TOO...

7

YES, YOU.

WHAT IF GOD COULD
USE EXACTLY WHAT
WE'VE GOT TO PULL
OFF SOMETHING BIG?

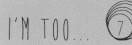

I walked away

from the opportunity for God to use me because I couldn't believe He could use me as I was. Let me tell you about the God I collided with who turned me right around from saying NOT ME, to instead saying, YES, YOU. He is a God who uses unlikely people. Throughout history God has used fraidy cats, punks, failures and big bad sinners with painful stories and sketchy pasts to change lives. God picks the least likely. If God chose to use the people we would choose...

HE IS A GOD WHO USES *unlikely people.*

● Goliath would still be bullying people. Instead God used an insecure, unequipped, young man who stepped up and didn't let insecurity in what he didn't have get in the way of what he was called to do. God used David to pelt an oppressive monster straight square in the eyes with a mere pebble to rescue His people. **1 Samuel 17**

● The Israelites would still be slaves for Pharaoh, the Red Sea never would have parted and we would be missing one of the best kids' movies ever (The Prince of Egypt) if Moses would have let his stutter and disability determine what he was supposed to do with his life. Instead Moses allowed the call of God to be louder than his weakness and that saved a nation. **Exodus 3**

● Gideon's people would still be oppressed while he put his confidence in his sissy baby self. Instead, God found that unlikely wimp hiding in fear, peeing his own pants and God used him to set His people free! **Judges 6**

● The 5000, hungry humans would still be hangry but instead God chose to use an unlikely little boy's lunch to feed a small city. **John 6**

You can sit around until you're 95 saying

● I'm too young in my faith.

● I'm too much of a disappointment.

● I'm too stained.

● I'm too plain.

● I'm too different.

● I'm too weighed down with baggage.

● I'm too ungodly.

Reflect

How are you saying to yourself, "God can't use me to do great things because I'm too....?" Fill in the blanks with the words that echo your negative self talk:

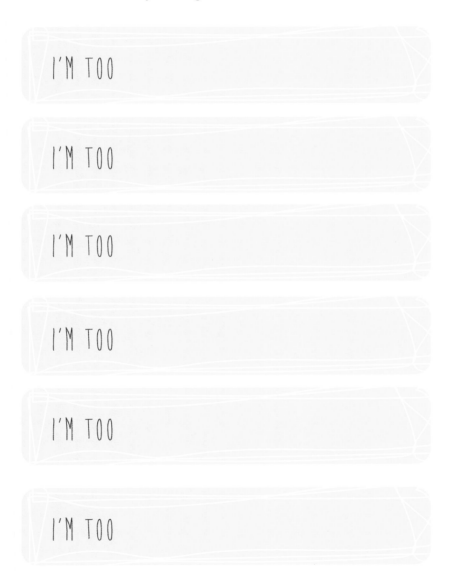

I'M TOO

I'M TOO

I'M TOO

I'M TOO

I'M TOO

I'M TOO

I'm too? God's too!

God's too big.

God's too supernatural.

God's too mighty.

God's too powerful.

God's too wise.

God's too amazing.

God's too *everything* you're too not.

If you think it's unlikely God can use you, you're in the right place. That's where Moses was at the burning bush. That's where Gideon was in the winepress. That's where Joseph was in a hole his brothers threw him in. Unlikely is God's middle name; it is there people will know His first. God uses unlikely people so we know it's Him and it's when you start to believe this, it will be you He uses! It's often when you're peeing your pants, when you're stuttering, when you're a harlot, when you're holding a bag of barley, it's in that kind of unlikeliness that God does the greatest things!

Read and Reflect

Examine the following passages to see examples of the contrast between "I'm too" and "God's too" in the lives of these Biblical figures.

1 Samuel 17

David's: " I'm too _____small_____ "

What does David realize about God that moves him from being stuck in his "I'm too" to instead trusting "God's too"?

In Verse 37 David realized the Lord rescued him from the paw of the lion and the paw of the bear and would rescue him from the hand of the Philistine.

Exodus 3:7-15

Moses' " I'm too _____ "

What did God say to Moses to invite him to move from "I'm too" to "God's too"?

Judges 6:1-16

Gideon's " I'm too _____ "

How did God reassure Gideon and help him move from "I'm too" to "God's too"?

John 6:1-13

The little boy's " I'm too _____ "

What did Jesus do to move this boy from thinking "I'm too inferior" to "God's too amazing"?

75

for more unlikely stories

of Moses and Gideon, read Exodus 3-4, 13:17-14:31 & Judges 6-8

From the Scriptures on the previous page, which person do you resonate with most?

How could that person's "I'm too" been a stumbling block for God to use them?

How is your "I'm too" getting in the way of God doing great things through you?

What do you like about a God who uses unlikely people?

Respond

Your "I'm too" becomes small in light of the majesty of "God's too." When you claim by faith who you believe God to be, who God is starts to overshadow who you have wrongly believed yourself to be. As you have spent time thinking about your "I'm toos," let's now respond by thinking about "God's toos."

God you are too big
God you are too incredible
God you are too gracious
God you are too...

Amen

CONFOUNDING

YES, YOU.

WHAT IF GOD COULD
USE EXACTLY WHAT
WE'VE GOT TO PULL
OFF SOMETHING BIG?

Read

²⁵ For the foolishness of God is wiser than human wisdom, and the weakness of God is stronger than human strength. ²⁶ Brothers and sisters, think of what you were when you were called. Not many of you were wise by human standards; not many were influential; not many were of noble birth. ²⁷ But God chose the foolish things of the world to shame the wise; God chose the weak things of the world to shame the strong. ²⁸ God chose the lowly things of this world and the despised things—and the things that are not—to nullify the things that are, ²⁹ so that no one may boast before him. ³⁰ It is because of him that you are in Christ Jesus, who has become for us wisdom from God—that is, our righteousness, holiness and redemption. ³¹ Therefore, as it is written: "Let the one who boasts boast in the Lord." **1 Corinthians 1:25-31**

Reread verse 26. As you think about what you were when you were called, take note of what these people were when they were called:

Rahab was a prostitute.

Matthew was a despised tax collector.

The dying man on the cross was a thief.

Paul was a persecutor of Christians.

Joseph was a lowly carpenter.

Lazarus was dead.

Reflect

If you were to be really honest with yourself, what impresses you about others? Is it their money, their power, their status, their talents, their smokin' hot bodies, something else?

What things that impress you, do you think impress God?

What things that impress you, do you think don't impress God?

Verse 26 suggests God doesn't call people based on human standards. If you had God's job of calling people to be used for amazing things in the world, what type of person would you not call?

Notice the repetition in verses 27 and 28.

God chose.
God chose.
God chose.

What does this repetition suggest?

What strikes you about a God who calls people who aren't "very impressive" to do amazing things?

The word shame in this passage is more accurately the word confound.

confound

verb | con.found | ken'found/
Cause surprise or confusion in (someone), especially by acting against their expectations.

synonyms: amaze, astonish, dumbfound, stagger, surprise, startle, stun, throw, shake, discompose, bewilder, bedazzle, baffle, mystify, bemuse, perplex, puzzle, confuse, mix up (something) with something else so that the individual elements become difficult to distinguish.

The word confound means to bring to ruin, destroy, baffle, frustrate, throw into confusion or perplexity. Scripture says God will confound you by who He uses. God will surprise you. God will not be predictable in His power. His power cannot be made sense by man. So then when He uses nitwits, depressed artists, recovering drug addicts and shy people, only God gets the props. "It must have been His power," people will say.

CONFOUNDING 8

"LET NOT THE WISE BOAST OF THEIR WISDOM OR THE STRONG BOAST OF THEIR STRENGTH OR THE RICH BOAST OF THEIR RICHES, BUT LET THE ONE WHO BOASTS BOAST ABOUT THIS: THAT THEY HAVE THE UNDERSTANDING TO KNOW ME, THAT I AM THE LORD, WHO EXERCISES KINDNESS, JUSTICE AND RIGHTEOUSNESS ON EARTH, FOR IN THESE I DELIGHT," DECLARES THE LORD.
JEREMIAH 9:23-24

Reflect

According to verses 27-28, what does God choose to use to confound people? Fill in the box below.

God chose the...	To confound the...
Foolish	
Weak	
Lowly, despised, things that are not	

How do you resonate with feeling

foolish?

weak?

lowly or despised?

How do you feel encouraged by the fact that God promises to use your feelings of foolishness, weakness and lowliness to confound those around you who are seemingly wise, strong, elevated, popular, a "big deal" or highly respected?

Why do you think God chose to confound the world by who and what He uses?

God confounded the world with His very self. And in fact, it is because of God showing up in the flesh as seemingly foolish, weak, and lowly, that many could not comprehend that Jesus was truly God in our midst.

Ruminate

²² Jews demand signs and Greeks look for wisdom, ²³ but we preach Christ crucified: a stumbling block to Jews and foolishness to Gentiles, ²⁴ but to those whom God has called, both Jews and Greeks, Christ the power of God and the wisdom of God.
1 Corinthians 1:22-24

Consider this...

To the Jews, they...."saw one who was meek and lowly, one who deliberately avoided the spectacular, one who served and who ended on a Cross—and it seemed to them an impossible picture of the Chosen One of God"[1] . . . "Christ crucified is a stumbling-block to the Jews. They could not get over it. They had a conceit that their expected Messiah was to be a great temporal prince, and therefore would never own one who made so mean an appearance in life, and died so accursed a death, for their deliverer and king."[2]

To the Greek, "the first characteristic of God was apatheia. That word means more than apathy; it means total inability to feel. The Greeks argued that if God can feel joy or sorrow or anger or grief it means that some man has for that moment influenced God and is therefore greater than he. So, they went on to argue, it follows that God must be incapable of all feeling so that none may ever affect him. A God who suffered was to the Greeks a contradiction in terms...The very idea of incarnation, of God becoming a man, was revolting to the Greek mind...To the thinking Greek the incarnation was a total impossibility. To people who thought like that it was incredible that one who had suffered as Jesus had suffered could possibly be the Son of God"[3] . . . "He was to the Greeks foolishness.

86

They laughed at the story of a crucified Saviour, and despised the apostles' way of telling it. They sought for wisdom. They were men of wit and reading, men that had cultivated arts and sciences, and had, for some ages, been in a manner the very mint of knowledge and learning. There was nothing in the plain doctrine of the cross to suit their taste, nor humour their vanity, nor gratify a curious and wrangling temper: they entertained it therefore with scorn and contempt. What, hope to be saved by one that could not save himself!"[4]

To the slave, "it was precisely this that was the glory of Christianity. In the Empire there were sixty million slaves. In the eyes of the law a slave was a 'living tool,' a thing and not a person at all. A master could fling out an old slave as he could fling out an old spade or hoe. He could amuse himself by torturing his slaves; he could even kill them. For them there was no such thing as marriage; even their children belonged to the master, as the lambs of the fold belonged not to the sheep but to the shepherd. Christianity made people who were things into real men and women, more, into sons and daughters of God; it gave those who had no respect, their self-respect; it gave those who had no life, life eternal; it told men that, even if they did not matter to other men, they still mattered intensely to God. It told men who, in the eyes of the world were worthless, that, in the eyes of God they were worth the death of his only Son."[5]

[1, 3, 5] William Barclay, The Letters to the Corinthians. Revised Edition. The Daily Study Bible Series, The Westminster Press; Revised Edition (1975)]

[2, 4] Matthew Henry, Matthew Henry's Commentary on the Whole Bible: Complete and Unabridged in One Volume, Hendrickson Pub; 2nd edition (1991)

> "CHRISTIANITY MADE PEOPLE WHO WERE THINGS INTO REAL MEN AND WOMEN, MORE, INTO SONS AND DAUGHTERS OF GOD; IT GAVE THOSE WHO HAD NO RESPECT, THEIR SELF-RESPECT; IT GAVE THOSE WHO HAD NO LIFE, LIFE ETERNAL; IT TOLD MEN THAT, EVEN IF THEY DID NOT MATTER TO OTHER MEN, THEY STILL MATTERED INTENSELY TO GOD"
> WILLIAM BARCLAY

The **Jews** were confounded by Jesus' meekness.

The **Greeks** were confounded by Jesus' suffering.

The **slaves** were overwhelmed by both. They knew once and for all that they were loved because God chose meekness and suffering for them.

Reflect

What about **you**? How do you feel about a God who looks seemingly foolish and lowly in our midst?

Even God Himself confounded the world with how He was used. We think it's going to be by our clout, our titles, our awesomeness, our cool factor, our magnetism, our put togetherness and our strength that changes lives. Who are we kidding? If God used His apparent foolishness, His weakness and His lowliness, why do we think He won't use ours? God will confound you.

Respond

God is a God who confounds. God wants to confound people with your life. Will you let Him? Write a prayer in response.

Barb

We encourage women to bravely and authentically tell their stories as they really are. We hope this "your story" meets you in yours...

When I heard those words no woman wants to hear, "You have breast cancer," I never imagined I was about to embark on the most exciting ride of my life. Earlier, feeling empty, I had prayed to God and asked Him if He could use even me in my senior years. I had no idea He was about to show me that not only would He use me, but He would use many others, including women into their nineties, to achieve His purposes and bring passion into many lives.

Complications from my mastectomy made immediate reconstruction impossible and I was left trying to figure out what I was going to do to appear "normal." The low point of my breast cancer journey was hearing the voice on the other end of the line telling me, "Oh, honey, I am so sorry but you can't put anything on that scar for at least six weeks." I was devastated.

My doctor indicated that many women are not happy with traditional breast prostheses. They can be hot, heavy, expensive and even require a special bra. He told me he had heard about this thing called a "knitted knocker" and asked if I could knit. Later, my friend Phyllis showed up at church with a "Victoria's Secret" bag. Inside, was the most beautiful "knitted knocker". It was soft and light and made by someone who cared. That gift of comfort and dignity literally changed my life and I immediately knew we needed to find a way to provide "knitted knockers" to doctor's offices so women could take them home and wear them in their most vulnerable time.

Soon I had a group of knitters and crocheters donating their time and materials to make breast prostheses. As popularity grew, it quickly became apparent we needed to do something to inspire and equip others to provide "knitted knockers" to their own communities. With over 50,000 mastectomies a year in the United States, the potential demand was way too much for one group to handle. How could we ever make these available for free to all who needed them?

God had a plan. While we thought we were just making lovely breast forms, God was actually taking our crafting talents and using them to show women everywhere they are loved and needed. Each handcrafted breast prosthesis was a tangible illustration to the recipient that a complete stranger cared for them. Not only that, the women making the knockers received the priceless gift of passion and purpose as they worked selflessly to provide for others, expecting nothing in return.

As Knitted Knockers began to receive publicity, a Dear Abby letter was published with such an overwhelming response that orders poured in at the rate of 250 an hour. Our Gmail account shut down at 9am because we had already reached our daily quota of 2,000 emails. When faced with the impossibility of filling all these orders, one volunteer said, "We can't do it. You have no one. All you have is a bunch of 70-year old women. You have no one." She was right. I cried out to God, "We have no one. What are we going to do?" But then I was reminded that God uses "nobodies" to do His greatest work

It was Gideon in the book of Judges who God asked to go out and defeat the Midianites. Gideon stated the obvious; he was the least of the least and the odds were impossible. But God had a plan. He said, *"Go in the strength you have…am I not sending you?"* **Judges 6:14** I thought about God's hand on us so far and His promise to instruct me in the way I should go. I thought about the strengths we have. I thought about Christel whose husband has dementia but finds joy in supporting our state suppliers all across the country. I thought about Laureen who had no money but baked her heart out to fundraise for a trip to Rwanda to train 30 women to provide knitted knockers in their country. There is Deborah, a retired domestic abuse hotline operator who handles our phone calls and listens to stories of pain, suffering and challenges with breast cancer. Candace has a daughter with addictions but she faithfully sends out support to our registered knitters and medical facilities. Ann is a grieving widow who finds solace and relief from her grief knowing she is making a difference with her time and talents. There is a 94-year-old woman in a nursing home who is so excited to be able to help some-one by crocheting and the class of '68 group comes in and stuffs thousands of knockers to send out. I realized that God had a plan and with Him using what little time and talents we had to offer, He would pull this off. I am still amazed when I remember that this group of "nobod-ies" sent out over 10,000 knitted knockers.

God took the pain and emptiness of one woman who thought she had very little to offer in her senior years, linked her with a bunch of willing hearts and used them to bring comfort and dignity to tens of thousands of women worldwide. All we had to offer was a little money, old bodies and the ability to knit. In an interview I did for

Good Housekeeping magazine, the interviewer said, "It's amazing what you have done, taking a great idea and your experience and expanding it to reach hundreds and thousands across the world." No, what is amazing is that God can use exactly what we have to pull off something really big. He took my shame and my desire to be used by Him to make a difference for so many people. My son asked me, "Mom, if you could go back and not have had breast cancer, would you, knowing what you know now?" My answer was, "No, I would not. I now have a passion and purpose far beyond my expectations and I can hardly wait to see what God has planned next."

Written by Barb Demorest
For more information about Knitted Knockers, go to
www.knittedknockers.org

WEAKNESS, WILLINGNESS AND PAIN

WHAT IF GOD COULD
USE EXACTLY WHAT
WE'VE GOT TO PULL
OFF SOMETHING BIG?

What does God use to do great things? We think God uses strength, experience, capability, power, resources, status, or fame….And He does. But even more than those, we see that over and over again in history, with His people, God uses humility, hardship, insecurities, stutterers, prisoners, family dysfunction, and grief. What God uses in a person's life to impact others is quite amazing.

He doesn't need your *put together* self.

He doesn't need your *résumé*.

He doesn't need your *accolades*.

He doesn't need your *trophies*.

He doesn't need your *popularity*.

He doesn't need your *approval* ratings.

God can use your *weakness*, your

willingness and your *pain*.

God uses weakness

Reflect

Where or how do you feel weak?

How does your "weakness" threaten your goals and dreams?

Why do you sometimes feel you need to display strength or power to do great things?

Read

⁹But he said to me (Paul), "My grace is sufficient for you, for my power is made perfect in weakness." Therefore, I will boast all the more gladly about my weaknesses, so that Christ's power may rest on me. ¹⁰ That is why, for Christ's sake, I delight in weaknesses, in insults, in hardships, in persecutions, in difficulties. For when I am weak, then I am strong. **2 Corinthians 12:9-10**

Hold onto these *promises:*

God's power is made *perfect* in *weakness.*

God uses our *weakness* for opportunities to show *His power.*

When you are *weak,* then you *are strong.*

God's power is made perfect in weakness.

God's power is shown not in strength. Not in armies. Not in CrossFit. Not in titles. Not in flashy lights. Not in beauty and perfection. Not in dolla dolla bills y'all. But in weakness.

You think that's ludicrous?

So is a little boy's lunch.
So is a rod.
So are 5 stones and a slingshot.
So is a prostitute with her long list of tricks and the pain that led her there.
So is God on a tree. Hanging there. For you…and me.

God's great rescue and impact on this Earth came through

humility. suffering. pain. wounds. weakness.

Reflect

If God's big impact came through what looked like weakness,
why would yours come through what looks like strength?

What do these often tell us we need to be to impact the world?

- hero characters in movies?

- worldly expectations?

- the education system?

- your own family of origin ideals?

- social media and magazines?

- your own experience with Christians and church?

- your own expectations and ideas you have had for yourself?

If you were to draw a picture of what the world tells you that you need to be like in order to do great things, what characteristics would you need to have?

— an ingenious brain

— lots o' money

God uses our weakness for opportunities to show His power. Weakness doesn't have the last word. God does. Weakness is God's agent displaying His power, God's best medium, God's opening act. Weakness makes way for God's character to be known and God's strength to be seen. Weakness becomes God's design studio, God's tool, God's plot to tell an even better story.

Weakness doesn't have the last word, unless of course, you let it

When you are weak, then you are strong.

Count on this. Don't just read it, claim it. Scripture says, it be so. God's promises aren't just for other people. They are for you too. When you are feeling doubtful, claim faith in the One who can do more than you can ask or imagine. When you are feeling tired and great energy is being required of you, count on the One who promises to be all that you need. When you are feeling unfit for the job, count on the One who can do the impossible in and through you. When you are lacking confidence in your capabilities, count on the One who holds all power to overshadow your weakness with His strength. When you are overwhelmed by what you are not, count on God to be what He is. Powerful.

That's what God does. When we are weak, He is strong. God shows up and does the unimaginable through us, like He did with the little boy, and it's then, in our weakness, that we know and can say without a shadow of a doubt, "God was here."

When facing the need to feed 5,000 people, how do you think this boy could have resonated with feeling weak? How then would he have had to believe God is strong?

What would it look like for you to trust God is strong in the places you now feel weak?

God uses willingness

I remember standing at a Collide event with a woman older than myself. She has a long list of accolades. She has traveled the continent doing international ministry. She has written a book. She has led countless people and led them well. She is the kind of woman I aspire to be. We were having a conversation about her possibly speaking at a Collide conference and this gifted, gorgeous, seventy-something-year-old woman said, in a defeated tone, "Willow, I don't think people want to hear what I have to say anymore. Our culture has a way of erasing the voices of little old ladies." I prayed for her and encouraged her to revisit her passionate belief that the gospel is intergenerational, that God intends for us to listen to one another.

Instead of staying in that place, she willingly handed God her lunch and He multiplied it! Donna started leading the Collide mentoring ministry which has created life-changing relationships, transforming marriages, trajectories and callings. It has been Donna's willingness that God has used to impact so many lives!

I love the passage of Scripture in **Isaiah 6:8** that says, *"Then I heard the voice of the Lord saying, 'Whom shall I send? And who will go for us?' And I said, 'Here am I. Send me!'"*

I often picture God hearing the cries of His people. He hears the cries of the widows in their grief. He hears the pangs of the hungry in their starvation. He hears the cries of the war-torn nations in their despair. He hears the cries of the refugees in their homelessness. He hears the cries of the abused in their well-kept secrets. He hears the cries of the children in their neglect. He hears His people's cries and He is a God who is looking for someone He can send to help.

All God needs is willingness and He can do the rest. I love that. You don't need to be a pastor, you don't need to be a genius, you don't need to be rich, you don't need to be charismatic or super spiritual. You can have a learning disability, you can have a sketchy past, you can do life in a wheelchair, you can wonder where your next paycheck is coming from, you can even have a brand spankin' new relationship with God and He can simply use your willingness, one that says, "Here I am. Send me."

Reflect

How do you see willingness play a role in the feeding of the five thousand? What did willingness look like on Philip's part?

Andrew's part?

The little boy's part?

Jesus' part?

What does willingness look like right now on your part?

WEAKNESS, WILLINGNESS AND PAIN — 9

God uses our pain

As I mentioned previously, long ago everything I saw in Jesus challenged my NOT ME's, so I turned right around with a certainty not in who I had been, but in who God was. It was that faith that walked me into vocational ministry. The pastors at the church where I got the internship threw me in with the wolves. No training. No Bible 101. No speech classes. So up on a stage, with a mic, just a few weeks in, I shared my story at the high school youth group. All I felt I had in my pocket was pain and Jesus meeting me there. A girl came up to me afterwards and said, "I know what it's like to hurt too. My dad beats me." The day I turned around and put my confidence in the greatness of what only God can do, was the beginning of experiencing greater things. My first lesson in God using me to do something great in another person's life was that God could use my pain to meet others in theirs.

Some time after giving that message my phone rang and a lawyer from the Midwest called to say she had a girl who was requesting to come and live with my husband and me. I said "Whaaaat?" The lawyer began to explain that the high school girl (who had approached me after the first message I ever preached) was on a plane and told her mom she had to go to the bathroom during a layover. She ran off and tried to escape her abuser and now wanted to live with me. There was nothing great about me, it was that God used my pain to engage hers.

She wanted my Rescuer. We wanted Him together.

Contrary to what I had assumed, God didn't use my "put togetherness", my cool factor, my perfect family tree, my Seminary degree or my strength, as we all expect He does. I had none of that. God started using the pain in my story to draw others towards His healing. This began to be my reality and my new story. And this is how the ministry of Collide began and how God continues to use it. For decades now, I have had the privilege of sitting with people who have trusted me with their stories. I have sat across from kids who have stabbed people, guys who are hooking up with anyone with a pulse on Craigslist, girls with eating disorders, high school runaways, suicidal men and women, beaten mothers, people possessed by the devil, prostitutes getting in cars to turn tricks, heroin addicts, parents grieving the loss of their children, orphans in third world countries, and college students trying to find God's purpose for their lives. I have sat across from them and for some out-of-this-world reason, I have experienced God using my brokenness to help others find His healing.

Read

²He had no beauty or majesty to attract us to him, nothing in his appearance that we should desire him. ³He was despised and rejected by men, a man of sorrows, and familiar with suffering. Like one from whom men hide their faces he was despised, and we esteemed him not. ⁴Surely he took up our infirmities and carried our sorrows, yet we considered him stricken by God, smitten by him, and afflicted. ⁵But he was pierced for our transgressions, he was crushed for our iniquities; the punishment that brought us peace was upon him, and by his wounds we are healed. **Isaiah 53: 2-5**

This passage in Isaiah describes what the Messiah, the One who could come and change the world, what He would look like. It's funny, even God Himself didn't use force or arrogance or the highest rung on a ladder or lots of letters after His name to do amazing things. He didn't use a perfect family line or a position of power or wealth or worldly ideals of strength to impact the world. God used not a crib but a manger. God used not a "because I told you so" authority, but an "I'll show you so humility." God used not a long line of Christian nobility but instead a family tree that was about as crooked as can be with harlots, ho's and heathens that birthed His DNA. God used not a throne, but a cross. God used not success but suffering. God used not a strong hand of punishment nor a power play, but instead He laid down His life in a salvation move that was well played.

What does God use to change the world? *Wounds.*

Reflect

What strikes you about a God who brings our healing through His pain?

WE HAVE A GOD WHO *enters brokenness* AND PURPOSES IT.

How do you think God could use your pain to bring help, relief or healing to others?

I love what Joseph said after he was betrayed and abandoned by his own brothers and then was used by God to reconcile his family and help a nation in famine because of that pain. He said, "*You intended to harm me, but God intended it all for good. He brought me to this position so I could save the lives of many people.*" **Genesis 50:20 NLT**

Some of us have been abandoned and instead of allowing God to use it, we are assuming we will be neglected and ditched and so we are still hiding out in a hole like the one Joseph was dropped into. Some of us have been hurt and we still live in fear and our fear is paralyzing our destiny. Some of us don't trust anybody because people haven't been trustworthy, and our trust issues are holding us back from great things. Some of us have been wounded by the Church and those wounds are keeping Jesus and His call on our lives at a distance. Some of us are sure our mess will keep following all our dreams, so we've stopped dreaming. Some of us have been told we don't have what it takes to do great things and we have started to believe it. We believe all those lies because our brokenness lies to us. But we have a God who enters brokenness and purposes it. We have a God who can take everything we've ever been through and He can, instead of writing us off, write the best stories with our pain. Our story of abuse can set free hundreds of kids who are being abused right now. Our messy divorce can be purposed to help others in theirs. Our struggle to like what we see in the mirror can come alongside a generation of young women and keep them from going down the agonizing road we once did.

How have you been harmed?

How can God use that for good?

How do you feel about God purposing your pain?

God does His greatest work through pain. His and ours.
Allow Him to MEET you in your brokenness and USE you there.

Respond

We have a God who will use our weakness, our willingness and our pain to do amazing things through our lives and in the lives of others. Claim His promises today by coming to Him with who you are, trusting Him for who He is....

God who is powerful, please be powerful in my weakness....

God who hears your people's cries, here I am, willing, please send me....

God whose wounds heal mine, please purpose my pain...

10 NOTHING WASTED

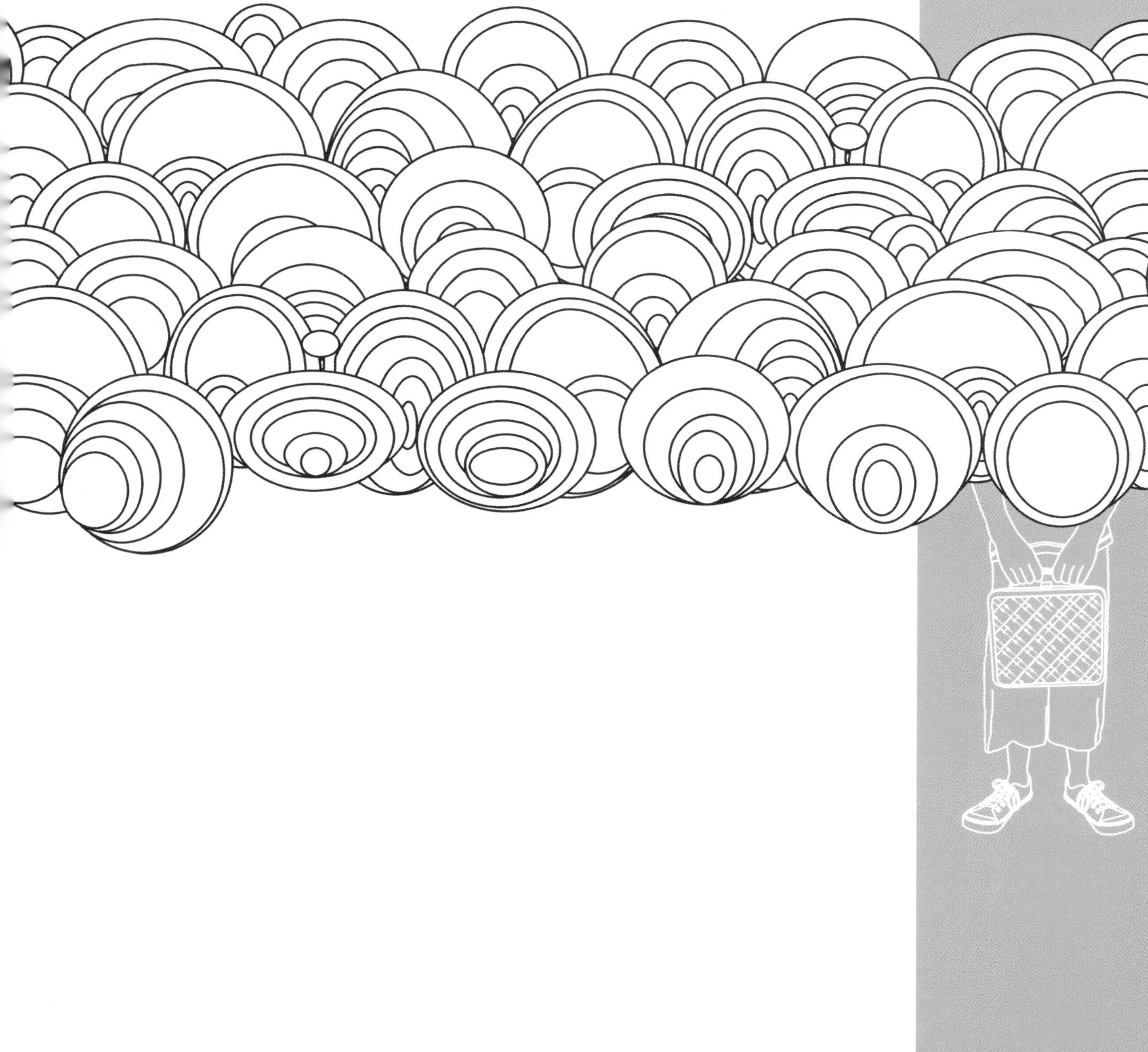

YES, YOU.

WHAT IF GOD COULD
USE EXACTLY WHAT
WE'VE GOT TO PULL
OFF SOMETHING BIG?

Read

¹²When they had all had enough to eat, he said to his disciples, "Gather the pieces that are left over. Let nothing be wasted." ¹³ So they gathered them and filled twelve baskets with the pieces of the five barley loaves left over by those who had eaten. **John 6:12- 13**

This story ends with the 5,000 once hungry humans now full on carbs with bread leftover. They had been following Jesus and now had witnessed a miracle and had their fill. They were in a state of repletion.

repletion

noun | re.ple.tion | \ri-ple-shen\

repletion is a condition of being completely full of something

The IVP Commentary says "It was a Roman custom always to have some food left over after a meal to indicate more than adequate provision. Jesus reveals himself as the ultimate host."[1] Jesus satisfied all His guests and there was an abundant surplus. Jesus is the host with the most. This isn't the first time God has provided just enough food if not more for people in want and in need. And the people gathered there that day on that hillside were quite familiar with these all too famous miracles where God had fed their people. Perhaps when they saw Jesus pull this big whopper of a miracle off, they wondered if the One their parents and their parents, and their parents, talked about was standing right here in their midst doing the very same thing.

Ruminate

Look up the following Scriptures:

- Exodus 16:11-18

- Deuteronomy 8:3

- Nehemiah: 9:15

- Psalm 78:24

- Psalm 105:38-40

- John 6:32-35

[1]Keener, C. S. (1993). The IVP Bible background commentary: New Testament (Jn 6:13). Downers Grove, IL: InterVarsity Press.

Reflect

Describe the character of a God who fed people in the desert, provided bread from heaven for their hunger, rained down what people needed in the Old Testament and now, here in the New Testament, shows up on a hillside and unnecessarily feeds people using a little boy's lunch.

What makes you believe that this God, who provided for the Israelites in the desert and did the same for the crowd on the hillside in John 6, won't do the same for you wherever you find yourself?

God is a God who has access to an abundance beyond what we even need. I think we often worry that God might not provide, God might not answer prayers, God might not have enough to go around and yet we have a God whose storehouses don't run dry. His pantry doesn't empty. His checks don't bounce. His gas tank doesn't need to be filled. His rivers don't run dry. We have a God whose abundance provides enough, if not more, for His people...

- They feast on the **abundance** of your house; you give them drink from your river of delights. **Psalm 36:8**

- You crown the year with your bounty, and your carts overflow with **abundance.** **Psalm 65:11**

- ...We went through fire and water, but you brought us to a place of **abundance.** **Psalm 66:12b**

- I will satisfy the priests with **abundance**, and my people will be filled with my bounty," declares the Lord. **Jeremiah 31:14**

- Mercy, peace and love be yours in **abundance.** **Jude 1:2**

Jesus Himself said in **John 10:10** *"The thief comes only to steal and kill and destroy; I have come that they may have life, and have it to the full."* The very reason for Jesus' coming to this messy place we call Earth and getting mess all over Himself was so that we each might experience life in its fullness. How beautiful is that? I love the line out of Mozart's Requiem, "Remember, merciful Jesus, that I am the cause of your journey."

We are the cause of Jesus' journey. He left perfection and entered imperfection for us. He stepped off His throne and came by way of a manger for us. The One who deserves all respect endured disrespect, mockery, flogging and being spat upon for us. Why? Why did Jesus come? He said it was so that you and I might have life abundant.

GOD HAS ACCESS TO AN *abundance* BEYOND WHAT WE EVEN NEED.

How cool is it that we have a God who came to Earth so that we would have abundant life and if we aren't experiencing that right now, He is a God who is....

still coming

still traveling

still moving

still parting seas

still gathering people

still doing miracles

still colliding so that you will experience the life you were made to live.

And here we see God still coming in **John 6** on an ordinary day in an extraordinary way. I love that there was an abundance in this collision, more than enough, because of course there was... that is what you get when you collide with Jesus, more than you even need. And how cool is it that Jesus' parting words with these people were "Let nothing be wasted."

Reflect

Would you say you are currently experiencing life in all its fullness? If not, what is keeping you from experiencing it?

God has come and is still coming for you in ways you can see and ways you can't, all so that you will live life to its abundance. How does this comfort you?

How often do you operate with an attitude of scarcity assuming there won't be enough of what you need?

In what ways do you need a God who has access to all abundance right now?

GOD IS STILL *colliding* SO THAT YOU WILL EXPERIENCE THE LIFE YOU WERE *made to live.*

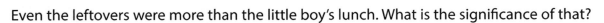

Even the leftovers were more than the little boy's lunch. What is the significance of that?

What do you think the leftovers told those present for this miracle?

Jesus takes a little boy's lunch, feeds 5000 and there is more left than they started with. Then He says, "Gather it up, nothing will be wasted."

Not your barley, not your pain.
Not your mistakes, not your victories.
Not your past, not your present.
Not your strength, not your weakness.

God wastes nothing.
God won't waste your inabilities, your wounds, your learning lessons, or your weak sauce lunch.
God will use all of it.

Reflect

Imagine God saying this to you personally, "Gather up the fragments of what is left. Nothing will be wasted. I will use it all." How does this encourage you?

If God can take something "inferior", multiply it to feed the masses, and still have more left than He started with, what steps of faith can you take to act on the belief that He can do this through your life?

Respond

Spend time writing your prayers to God today…

God, I come before you as the One who feeds and fills, and I pray…

God, I come before you as the One who has access to abundance and I pray….

God, I come before you as the One who came that I may have life to the full and I pray….

God, I come before you as the One who wastes nothing, and I pray….

Michelle

We encourage women to bravely and authentically tell their stories as they really are. We hope this "your story" meets you in yours...

We had made two cross country moves in 2 ½ years and I had no idea, given the nature of my husband's job, how many more were in our future. I found myself making a conscious decision. In order to protect my heart, from that point on, I would sit on the sidelines. Who knew how long we would live in this new home and just thinking about the heartbreak of once again saying goodbye to treasured friends and letting go of a fulfilling ministry left me feeling weary. It would just be easier, I reasoned, to hold back and not give too much of myself away. But all that holding back only left me feeling empty, lonely and without purpose.

One day, while sitting in a Bible study where we were discussing John 6, a new thought occurred to me. I think I've heard the story of Jesus multiplying the loaves and fish so many times that, sometimes, I forget to stop and think how truly incredible this miracle is. When they had all had enough to eat, Jesus' disciples gathered 12 baskets full of leftovers. This means each disciple ended up with his own basket full of provision from the Lord, each held a literal basket of miracles.

I wonder, did they ever think about those baskets later in life? Did they remember the weight of the baskets in their arms and the feeling of awe as they marveled at what they had witnessed that day on the hillside? Did the thought of those baskets help them through the hard times as they were encouraged by the awesome power of Jesus?

What about my basket, what amazing things has God done for me?

He has given me loving, encouraging friends all over this great country. He has introduced me to the most remarkable women and allowed me to learn from them as I watch how they live their lives. He has sustained my family throughout all of our moves and used the experiences to draw us even closer as a family. He has led us to welcoming neighborhoods and churches. He has helped my children learn the value of resiliency. He has given me the opportunity to have a variety of ministry opportunities. He has seen me through the loss of a parent, financial worries, medical emergencies and countless other personal miracles.

So why do I often forget about my basket? I guess it's not all that surprising I do this and maybe you do too. Even some of the very same people who had their fill of the loaves and fish came looking for Jesus the following day, asking for a miraculous sign to prove He was who He said He was. SERIOUSLY???? I often delude myself into thinking if I had lived when Jesus walked the Earth, been one of the multitudes he fed and seen the things they were blessed to see, I would never doubt who Jesus is. But the truth is, I don't need to have lived in those times; I can see Jesus all around me. I have an overflowing basket of amazing things He has done in my life and still I often forget who He is. I forget He can do immeasurably more than all I can ask or imagine.

So that day in Bible study, while sitting off to the side, intentionally distancing myself from the others, afraid to let anyone in, I was challenged to take hold of the basket God has given me, to feel the weight of it deep in my soul, to remember when I am tired and hurt and unwilling to open my heart, that it is in those very places where Jesus makes Himself known to me and fills me with more than I need. Jesus is my provider, my sustainer, my portion. He overflows my basket with His goodness. How could I forget that? Why would I put a lid on my basket and say, "no more"? Instead, I made a new decision. It was time to say, "Yes." Yes to friendships, even if it will hurt to say goodbye. Yes to ministry, even if I may have to leave it behind someday. Yes to going deeper and farther than I ever imagined He would take me. Yes to Jesus.

Written by Michelle Holladay

MAKE IT COUNT

YES, YOU.

WHAT IF GOD COULD
USE EXACTLY WHAT
WE'VE GOT TO PULL
OFF SOMETHING BIG?

On the sidelines of our sons' football game, another mom said to me "I want to make my cancer count." I realized that day, she watched football games differently than I do. Julia watched them like she wasn't sure how many more she would get to watch. Just her presence pierced mine. I got her. She was my age. She was married to a faithful, good man. She was a mom and loved her kids like crazy and probably wanted to watch them graduate and get married and grow old. A few years before our conversation at the football game she was diagnosed with stage 4 cancer and by the time I met her, it had already spread into her breasts, lungs and even her spine.

When she was at the Cancer Care hospital, apparently a woman decked out in Harley Davidson gear challenged her: "We're not dying from cancer, we're living with it." Julia's response to her diagnosis was, "Could I lie in bed all day? Yes, but that's not living with cancer, that's dying from it." This kind of attitude led Julia to start an organization in the midst of her fight called Team Julia which has been helping fund a cure for cancer and helping other cancer patients pay their hospital bills. (For more information, please visit teamjulia.org)

Julia ended up saying goodbye to her children and her husband and is now living in the perfect place where there is no cancer, no grieving children and no longings cut short. Amid the grief, all those who knew her can say without a shadow of doubt that she truly made her cancer count. She used her pain and suffering for Glory. I am in awe of how she chose to live and die.

At her funeral, a lot of the boys on the county champ football team showed up wearing their green and white jerseys just to say to their friend who lost his mother, "We are on your team in victory and in loss." Sitting in the waft of "It is well with my soul" and hearing countless stories of this woman who lived her entire life for Jesus, I started to see how all these people had come together and were being invited to come to Jesus and allow Him to make their lives count like she did.

Julia invited us into something we ALL want. I think within each one of us resides a deep desire to live a life of great purpose. We want to make our life count.

Reflect

How do you find yourself desiring to make your life count?

If you knew your time was running out, how do you picture living differently than you do now?

TO READ MORE ABOUT THIS STORY (life, death, wins and losses), PLEASE VISIT OUR BLOG AT WECOLLIDE.NET/BLOG

I Think we are born with a place inside of us that is made to impact this world. No matter who we are, what age, what race, what gender, what socio-economic status, we all want this. I think every person on the hillside there, listening to Jesus that day in **John 6** wanted this. We all want our lives to count. I think this place in us goes so deep, that if not filled, we begin to pace the halls of life. If empty, this place in us is begging for more and we find ourselves starving for contentment. This desire for purpose is so strong that if not satiated, we can actually end up feeding it with ugly, awful, no good, emotional junk food. Junk food like TV and clothes and the Kardashians and Cheetos. The kind of junk food that rots our soul. I think we all yearn to make our lives count, yet we let so many other things count.

- **We let our past count:** We think only people with Sunday school, mission trips and Bible college on their résumé can apply for the work of doing big Godlike assignments. We think our track record is pretty weak and God won't want us on His team. So, we keep letting our past determine our present. And yet God is a God who says, "Let me determine your present and your future. The past rests in my forgiveness." He says this, and yet we continue to give our past way too much power.

- **We let our weakness count:** We let our inadequacies get the best of us. We convince ourselves that "we aren't enough" to really make a big difference. There is nothing great about us. We are lacking, broken, quirky, boring, understated, old, and weak. These lies boss our lives around every day.

- **We let "I'm not her" count:** We sit around and look at other women and think, why try? I'm not Oprah, I'm not Mother Theresa, I'm not Amy Poehler.

  "I'm not her"

  that girl whose presence we allow to tell us what we don't have, more than what we do. You know you can spend your whole life imprisoned by the fact that you aren't her and her and her. And then what? I say, "Be you, not her."

- **We let our season in life count:** We spend so many seasons of our lives seeing all the obstacles in the way of why we can't do what we want to do! In college we say, "When I'm out of college." When we get married we say, "When things settle." When we first get into our career we say, "Maybe later." When we have babies we say, "When they're older." When we are running every which way driving our teens around we say, "When I'm an empty nester." When we're empty nesters we say, "If I woulda, coulda, shoulda." Do you think God is surprised by your season? Who is it to say you can't have an impact in college? Why are you waiting for a piece of paper to make it count? Who is to say you can't have an impact as a mom? Why are you waiting until your kids are older? Retirees, who's to say your days to change the world have retired? Why can't you change the world right now? Don't wait for purpose. Purpose waits for you. Just show up.

BE you, NOT her.

We let self count: Let's be honest, we are often focused on us, our plans, our path, our promotion, our job, our vacation, our body, our stress. When we live like this, our impact can't be measured farther than our own nose. All those things we focus on can count: our plans, our job, our vacation. But in all those things, is the focus on you or your impact? You impact others when others are your focus.

We let only BIG things count: We overcomplicate impact. We think, "I have to do something huge." And what can I do? I can make a mean chili. I can plant a garden. I can paint. I can do math. Last time I checked, Jesus healed a blind man with spit and mud. He fed thousands with one boy's lunch. God used a staff to show people who is boss. I am not sure you need much more than a broom, a paint-brush or a pot of soup for God to use you to do something BIG.

We let fear count: What if I fail? What if I succeed? What if people laugh? "What if's" will find you at the end of your life asking, "What if I would not have asked what if?"

We let the haters count: We believe them when they say ,"You don't have what it takes. You aren't smart enough, pretty enough, strong enough. You need more of this. You need more of that." We give the naysayers, the negative Nellies, the critics and the haters voices more power than God's voice.

Reflect

Which of these things are you letting count? Fill in the table with the ways you are letting these things count:

Past	Weakness	"I'm not her"	Season
Self	Only "Big" Things	Fear	Haters

How is letting these things count getting in the way of making your life count?

What if the little boy with the little lunch let these count? What if he would have let Philip's "this is impossible" count? What if he would have let "fear" count? What if he would have let his "season" in life count?

Ruminate

Judas let _____selfish gain_____ count. **Matthew 26:14-15**

The rich young ruler let _____ count. **Mark 10:17-22**

Samson let _____ count. **Judges 16:1-5**

Joseph's brother's let _____ count. **Genesis 37:18-36**

Martha let _____ count. **Luke 10:38-42**

The Pharisees let _____ count. **Mark 2:15-17**

Philip let _____ count. **John 6:5-7**

Me, I let _____ count.

God doesn't value what we make count. God doesn't seem to count selfish gain, worldly treasures, lust for pleasure, envy of others, busyness, man's religious rules, and impossibilities. A lot of the characters we just ruminated on missed out on the call, the impact, or the assignment God had for them because they let things count that God doesn't. Some of them even missed out on God Himself because they allowed other things to take precedence over His presence. God couldn't use the rich young ruler to bless the poor because he chose to make his wealth count more than his influence. God couldn't get a word in edgewise to encourage or teach or call Martha because in the moment, she chose to make her preparations count more than Jesus. God couldn't use Philip to feed the 5000, hangry humans because he chose to make man's impossibilities greater than God's greatness that makes all things possible. We often let so many things count in our lives by allowing them to have the say, to boss us around, to rule our desires, to take over our schedules and to infringe on what really matters. God desires for our lives to count, to matter, to be meaningful, to be purposed, to impact the world around us.

When we let so many of these things count, our lives don't. These things get the best of us.

They win.
They tell the story.
They have the impact.

Reflect

What are the things that are getting the best of you and having an impact on you rather than you having an impact on the world?

God isn't concerned about us not being able to do BIG things. He is concerned about people who need BIG things. Making an impact is not about who you are or who you aren't. Making an impact is about people in need. God always shows up on people's scenes and calls them because people are crying out. When God showed up to Gideon in a winepress and called that little wimp a warrior, was it about Gideon? No, it was about the Israelites who were being oppressed by the Midianites. When God was in a burning bush getting Moses' attention, was it about Moses? No! It was about God's people in misery in Egypt. God shows up to Gideon and Moses and everyone else He has used to do BIG things because He hears His people crying out. God is moved by the cries of people and He wants you to be too.

Reflect

Are you moved by the cries of people? If so, what are you actively doing about it?

You don't know how long "it" lasts...the impact you get to have on your kids, your spouse, your neighbors, your co-workers, your barista, your pastor, your friends, your frenemies or your enemies...this is what matters most. When we make our lives count, God will use it to change our world. Sometimes it's so overwhelming to think about being called to change the world. The world is a very big place. But I am only called to change "my world" wherever my world is. And you are called to change "your world" wherever your world is. And if you and she and him and her and I all change our piece of the world, then together, God can use us to greatly impact our world.

There may be nothing sweeter than being a part of what God is doing. That day on that hillside might have been the greatest day of that boy's life and potentially catapulted him into a faith to believe God can do anything and if God can do anything, then what could stop him from doing more big, amazing, awesome things in his future? There may not be a greater experience in life than to tap into God purposing you. There is no better feeling than to make your life count for the reason God gave it to you in the first place.

I still have to fight the NOT ME that gets in the way of my life really counting. I'm still the girl with no Bible 101, no speech class, and a big booty. How could God use me? I had to speak at a retreat recently and I was so tired, had little in my cup to pour out and the last thing I wanted to do was leave my family for the weekend. We have been running at a crazy pace and God is doing all these great things, but I often feel overwhelmed and unqualified for all that He is doing. My friend Kelli came with me to pray over the weekend. As we drove to the retreat, I was feeling fatigued and faithless, like, what could God do through me that was going to impact all these women I was about to speak to? I spent the weekend giving these women the little I felt like I had.

I prayed after my last message. We said our goodbyes and, if I'm honest, I was so ready to go home and get in sweats and cuddle my kids and sleep that I was almost running out of there but trying to look like I wasn't. And wouldn't you know it, right when we were walking out the door a woman stopped me. She expressed thanks and then began to share. She was deeply sad and shocked me with the seriousness of her story. When she said, "I want to die. I want to go take some pills and go to sleep and never wake up again," I gulped, as if I could be hearing her incorrectly. She just kept saying the same thing in different ways and it became apparent that this woman was suicidal and seriously considering ending her life. All of a sudden, my tiredness and longing to be home took a back seat. I set my bags down, my plans down and my butt down and sat next to her as she wept.

Here I found myself as that same girl I was 20 years ago, with pain in my pocket and a God who meets me there. What I had or what I didn't, neither could help this woman. She needed something so beyond me. This woman wanted to give up her life. We needed a Supernatural, God-sized miracle. Kelli and I began to fight for her life. We fought for her will to live. We fought for her hope and her faith. We handed her to Jesus and her community, so they could help her get the help she needed to live the life God dreams for her. All I knew, driving back home that night, was that my NOT ME's do nothing for this world. My YES YOU's are all I've got, and all God needs.

That woman's life counts, and God gave my life the opportunity to count by helping hers. So many things get in the way of us making our life count and yet when we do make it count, there is no greater way to live. My friend Julia made her life and death count just like her Lord Jesus and I hope to do the same. Will you make your life count too? Together we can change the world.

OUR *not me's* DO NOTHING FOR THIS WORLD. OUR *yes you's* ARE ALL WE'VE GOT, AND ALL GOD NEEDS.

Respond

Count three things you can do this week to make your life count that you have been putting off or avoiding because you have been making other things count.

Take some time to ask God to bless your intentionality in these three things as you lean into Him to really make all that you do have purpose and impact.

HAND IT OVER

12

WHAT IF GOD COULD
USE EXACTLY WHAT
WE'VE GOT TO PULL
OFF SOMETHING BIG?

God will use what we have, but we have to hand it over. Eventually, the boy had to hand over his lunch. Eventually, he had to decide. Would he hold onto his fish and loaves and laugh off the whole suggestion? Would he hoard his lunch? Would he take Andrew's encouragement as mockery?

Somehow this boy got to the place where he held out his measly lunch, knowing it wouldn't feed thousands and handed it to Jesus, trusting Jesus could do something with what he had. Handing over what we have to God is quite potentially one of the greatest acts of faith we can ever make. We have a God who does big, amazing, supernatural, miraculous things. But we have to hand over what we have, and when we do, you won't believe the amazing things He does.

Reflect

What does Jesus have that you don't, that enables Him to do with your life what you cannot?

Read

[14] *After the people saw the sign Jesus performed, they began to say, "Surely this is the Prophet who is to come into the world."* [15] *Jesus, knowing that they intended to come and make him king by force, withdrew again to a mountain by himself.*
John 6:14-15

the disciples, the crowd, the little boy, they had all seen Jesus do what no man could. They witnessed a miracle. All the signs pointed towards Jesus being Someone who could do what only God could. Right? Because what man can take some Wonder bread and some sardines and feed the multitudes? No man or woman I know can do that. I wish. Every morning that I have to make school lunches for my kids, I wish I could thank God and boom, peanut butter and jelly

HANDING OVER *what we have* TO GOD IS QUITE POTENTIALLY ONE OF THE GREATEST *acts of faith* WE CAN EVER MAKE.

sandwiches all whipped up ready for the kids to walk out the door! But clearly, I cannot do this because I am limited by my own humanity.

This statement in verse 14 that they began to utter about Jesus being "the Prophet", was a confession of faith, believing that He was the "One who was to come." See, these people had been waiting for a very long time for the One, the Prophet, the Messiah to come and make everything better, to redeem all wrongs, to heal all pain and to bring about victory where they had experienced great defeat.

Read

The Lord your God will raise up for you a prophet like me (Moses) *from among you, from your countrymen, you shall listen to him.* **Deuteronomy 18:15 NASB**

Hundreds of years prior to Jesus coming, a "prophet" had been prophesied to come and now they were seeing Him with their very own eyes. The Bible Knowledge Commentary says about **John 6**, "Seeing this miraculous sign ...the people recalled Moses' prediction that a Prophet like him would arise... Moses had fed the people. Moses had led them out of bondage. Jesus had fed the people. Jesus could lead the people out of the hated Roman bondage." [1]

People had been waiting for someone to come and lead them out of bondage for hundreds of years. Seeing what Jesus could do, the crowd who had had their fill of carbs and fish now hoped Jesus would be the One to lead them out of their own slavery.

The songwriter, Isaiah, whose own name means, "The Lord saves" wrote about a Savior, a Yahweh, A Messiah who was on His way and the lyrics describe what this One would look like. In **Isaiah 53**, the song goes a little like this: *He had no beauty or majesty to attract us to him, nothing in his appearance that we should desire him. [3] He was despised and rejected by mankind, a man of suffering, and familiar with pain. Like one from whom people hide their faces he was despised, and we held him in low esteem. [4] Surely he took up our pain and bore our suffering, yet we considered him punished by God, stricken by him, and afflicted. [5] But he was pierced for our transgressions, he was crushed for our iniquities; the punishment that brought us peace was on him, and by his wounds we are healed.*

700 years after this song hit the airwaves, the Savior, God in the flesh, Jesus, as prophesied, entered life with people and moved them as no music ever has (as we see in this collision where He uses one little boy's lunch to bless a hillside of thousands.) But here's the thing about Jesus... Jesus didn't look like people thought He would and Jesus didn't lead like people thought He should.

[1]Blum, E. A. (1985). John. In J. F. Walvoord & R. B. Zuck (Eds.), The Bible Knowledge Commentary: An Exposition of the Scriptures (Vol. 2, p. 294). Wheaton, IL: Victor Bc

Reflect

Why do you think Jesus didn't want to be a king by force?

Jesus didn't look like people thought He would and Jesus didn't lead like people thought He should. How do you think this affected people's experience of Jesus?

How do you think you expect Jesus to look or lead in a way He doesn't and how do you think your unmet expectations affect your experience of Him?

Ruminate

Read what these commentators say about Jesus who would not be a king by force:

> "Jesus did not need an earthly crown, and he certainly did not come to lead a military expedition. So instead of acceding to their desires, he headed for the hills and left them with their unfulfilled political expectations."[2]
> **The New American Commentary**

THESE PEOPLE INTENDED AS VERSE 15 SAYS "TO MAKE HIM KING BY FORCE"

BUT JESUS *would have none of it.*

[2]Borchert, G. L. (1996). John 1–11 (Vol. 25A, p. 257). Nashville: Broadman & Holman Publishers.

"Although Jesus is indeed king, his kingdom is not of this world, and so he would not let himself be forced into being made the kind of king these people were looking for."[3]
A Handbook on the Gospel of John

"As if it were to be of this world, and he must appear with outward pomp, a crown on his head, and an army at his foot; such a king as this they would make him, which was as great a disparagement to his glory as it would be to lacquer gold or paint a ruby. Right notions of Christ's kingdom would keep us to right methods for advancing it."[4]
Matthew Henry's commentary on the whole Bible

To force Jesus to be king, to rule and reign to advance our purposes, to further our agenda, to lead as we want Him to, would be as great a disaster as "to lacquer gold or paint a ruby." To want God to be what we think He ought to be is like destroying a pure gem by painting it with acrylic, like covering gold in plastic, like taking what is perfect and good and glossing it with manmade falsehood, slime, ruin and cow dung, all because we think somehow we know what is right and true and best.

Jesus wouldn't be forced to be anything He wasn't, and He is still that way. He'll run for the hills before He will allow us to make Him out to be something He is not. You cannot force Jesus to be your king the way you want a king, any more than you can paint a ruby and try to sell it for its original value. Jesus wants to be known for who He is. Jesus wants to be King ruling and reigning in power in the way this King knows best to rule and reign. He will not bow down to man's charm, man's man-made religious rules, man's armies, man's hierarchies, man's plans or man's ideas of who God is.

Sure, this offer to be King could have been a major moment of enticement for Jesus. He could have been given the throne, the power, the honor, the slaves, the sexy women, the bountiful feasts, the wealth, and the bling. But this king knew He couldn't have the kingdom without the cross, nor could He be your king without taking on your suffering. His reign would come but it would look different than people would expect. It would look and sound like Isaiah's song. This king would be mocked, whipped, afflicted, pierced, and punished.

[3] Newman, B. M., & Nida, E. A. (1993). A handbook on the Gospel of John (p. 183). New York: United Bible Societies.
[4] Henry, M. (1994). Matthew Henry's commentary on the whole Bible: complete and unabridged in one volume (p. 1950). Peabody: Hendrickson

E. A. Blum says of this moment where Jesus performed the miracle of feeding the 5,000, "This marks the highpoint of Jesus' popularity and a great temptation for Him. Could He have the kingdom without the Cross? No. Jesus' kingdom would be given to Him by the Father. It will not come from this world. The path of the Father's will lies in another direction. Before He can be the reigning Lion of Judah, He must be the Lamb who bears the sin of the world." [5]

These people's offer for Jesus to become king was motivated by their own personal gain for bread and miracles more than it was their personal recognition of who Jesus is.

Reflect

How does your own motivation for personal gain of bread and miracles often get in the way of you wanting God for who God is?

Isaiah 53:5 says, "By His wounds we are healed." What do you think about Jesus that He chose to forego the temptation of being crowned king because He knew His kingdom would come through enduring our pain on the cross?

What if Jesus would have given in and chosen the world's way of kingly rule?

"BEFORE HE CAN BE THE REIGNING LION OF JUDAH, HE MUST BE THE *Lamb* WHO BEARS THE SIN OF THE WORLD." E.A. BLUM

[5]Blum, E. A. (1985). John. In J. F. Walvoord & R. B. Zuck (Eds.), The Bible Knowledge Commentary: An Exposition of the Scriptures (Vol. 2, p. 294). Wheaton, IL: Victor Books.

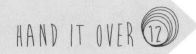

How can Jesus' denial of self in the face of the world's temptation to be "great" encourage us when we face the same?

All these people on this hillside had to have wondered who this Jesus was. Who do you think this collision told them He was?

When we collide with Jesus and see him take a little boy's lunch and feed five thousand people, when we see him touch lepers no one else would touch and cleanse them, when we see Him restore sight to the blind and heal women who had been hemorrhaging for years, we can't help but want more of what He does. But do we want more of who He is? Seeing Jesus in our midst makes us wonder... who is this Jesus? Is He merely a great teacher, a great host or a magician?

The great poet, novelist, academic and lay theologian, CS Lewis challenges us, "I am trying here to prevent anyone saying the really foolish thing that people often say about Him: I'm ready to accept Jesus as a great moral teacher, but I don't accept his claim to be God. That is the one thing we must not say. A man who was merely a man and said the sort of things Jesus said would not be a great moral teacher. He would either be a lunatic — on the level with the man who says he is a poached egg — or else he would be the Devil of Hell. You must make your choice. Either this man was, and is, the Son of God, or else a madman or something worse. You can shut him up for a fool, you can spit at him and kill him as a demon or you can fall at his feet and call him Lord and God but let us not come with any patronizing nonsense about his being a great human teacher. He has not left that open to us. He did not intend to."[6]

If Jesus is only a teacher, how did He turn water into wine, heal dropsy and take cheapo bread and feed the multitudes? You can say, "That was thousands of years ago." I beg to differ. Get coffee with people who are seeing Jesus show up in their lives at this present time and ask them to share their stories. Jesus is taking our pain and using it to minister to people on the hillsides. That's what Collide is- a movement of broken, imperfect, messy, real people running into Jesus and the more they collide with Him, the more their

 [6] Lewis, C.S. Mere Christianity. Harper One, 2015

lives are being transformed. Jesus is resurrecting marriages that were dead. Jesus is showing up and bringing healing to wounds that have been bleeding for way too long. Jesus is meeting people who have been sweeping pain under the rug for decades and they, with a raw authenticity, are running into His invitation of wholeness. Jesus is infusing people who wanted to end their lives with immense hope that is giving them the will to live. Young girls who cut because they think they deserve pain are running into the One who takes on all of our shame and these girls are being freed up to love themselves! Jesus is doing 180's in the lives of those who had been going in a destructive direction and now they are traveling in the way of their destiny. Jesus is calling people who thought they had very little to offer and He is using them in ways beyond their wildest dreams to impact this world.

Jesus' miracles are alive and well!

You just have to sit on the hillside long enough where He is teaching and the next thing you know, you, yourself will run into Him and see the amazing power He has to take what little we have to bring to the table and make it big. His power, His healing, His bread, His goodness, His miracles are available for you too. They haven't expired. They aren't for only the really "spiritual" people. They aren't antiquated. They aren't biased. They aren't just for those who have their stuff together. Jesus wants to meet you on any hillside you find yourself and show you that He is Here, Present, Dwelling, Powerful, Mighty, Good and With you.

In John 6, the crowd sat under His teaching but also observed His miracles. They must have thought "He cannot be mere man, yet here He is like man, in the flesh, doing what only God can." Jesus' move in our midst invokes a response. Like CS Lewis so poignantly states, you either decide He is God in our midst, a tremendous fool or a demon. If He be the Lord, how can you not but collide with Him and fall at your feet in awe and wonder wanting more of His rule, reign and redemption in your life and our world, while believing upon Him to be able to pull it off?

Reflect

Who do you believe Jesus to be?

> "YOU CAN SHUT HIM UP FOR A FOOL, YOU CAN SPIT AT HIM AND KILL HIM AS A DEMON OR YOU CAN FALL AT HIS FEET AND CALL HIM LORD AND GOD, BUT LET US NOT COME WITH ANY PATRONIZING NONSENSE ABOUT HIS BEING A GREAT HUMAN TEACHER. HE HAS NOT LEFT THAT OPEN TO US. HE DID NOT INTEND TO."
> C.S. LEWIS

If He be your Lord, why do you often struggle to believe that He can do through you what He did through the little boy?

How can you crown Jesus as King of your life? What does Jesus need to rule and reign that you've been trying to rule and reign yourself?

Who do you think the boy in John 6 thought Jesus was after He performed this miracle?

What is the "action" that this boy did to experience God using his life for something amazing?

All this boy did was hand over his lunch. Notice, he didn't talk, he didn't move, he didn't argue or stomp his feet, he didn't doubt, and he didn't hide. This lad very simply handed over what he had to the only One who could take it and do something beyond what he could. You can hand your turkey and cheese over to a friend and they can eat it, but they can't feed the crowd with it. You can hand over your phở to a spiritual mentor and they can add basil and lime juice for you, but they can't perform a miracle with it. You can hand over your dreams to man but what more can they do than listen, dream or pray? But with God, you can hand over your gifts and your weaknesses, your story and your experiences, your learning lessons and your struggles and God can take all of what you've got to pull off something big.

It's all about WHO you're handing what you've got.

this boy handed over his inferior lunch, knowing it wouldn't feed the crowd and handed it to Jesus, trusting Jesus had the power to do something with what he had. Handing over what we have to God is the greatest act of faith that leads to the greatest lives lived. But the handoff is up to you. And it's not a one-time deal. We have to keep handing to God what we have. Mondays, Tuesdays, Wednesdays... morning, noon and night...in victory and in defeat...in love and out...in fear and with courage. All of it, all the time. You can hold what you have and hoard it for yourself. You can doubt God can do much with it. You can be afraid of the onlookers if it fails. Or you can hand it over to Jesus who can take it and do something out of this world.

You want to change the *world?*

You want to impact a *generation?*

You want to live out your God destined *dreams?*

You can! Your confidence needs to be not in yourself and what you can or can't do.

Your *confidence* needs to be in Christ.

Lay down your *insecurities* and your *pride*.

Lay down your *failures* and your *past*.

Lay down your *wounds*.

And pick up *the greatness of Jesus Christ*. You can be confident, He is all you need to do great things!

Lay down YOUR CONFIDENCE AND YOUR INSECURITIES AND PICK UP THE GREATNESS OF JESUS CHRIST.

Respond

God does amazing things when we hand Him what we have. Let's end our time colliding in this study by taking the opportunity to do just that. Take a moment to, by faith, hand to God all that you are. I actually want to invite you, like I did the day I gave my life to Christ, and many times since, to extend your hands out as if you are handing God what you have, and pray along with me…

God, I give you what I have and what I don't. God, I give you all my *not me's.* I give you my doubts and my failings. I give you my insecurities and I give you my talents. I give you my past my present and my future. I give you my dreams too. I hand them to you and ask that you would take them and do something amazing with me. I hand you my life. Waste nothing, God. Please replace my NOT ME 's with *yes you's*

I am trusting you, God, with all that I have and all that I don't. Jesus, I trust that you will use my life for greatness. You are the Bread of life that fills me. You are the Healer of my wounds. You are the power I don't have. You are the King I need. You are the Lord I want. Yes, you, Jesus. *Amen*

come

collide.

with us

we have more ways you can collide

with Jesus at wecollide.net

or find us on

Acknowledgements

This project was a collective work of some amazing women getting together and trusting God could use the sum of what we have to do something big. I am so very grateful for these women who poured out their energy, leaned into their giftings, gave of their time, and made great sacrifices to craft this project and get it into the hands of those we believe it will impact. God calls His people the Body, and as I like to say, God gave Collide one hot body! These beautiful women are the hands and feet, the heart and mind, the lungs and mouthpiece being used to bless the world around them and for that, I am truly grateful. There is nothing greater than together handing God what we have and seeing what He can do!   - Willow

Willow Weston, Author   *Willow's life is full of crazy, unexpected, broken and beautiful moments that have given way to incredible healing both in her own life and now others. Willow is a sassy, fun, word nerd. She is a spelling bee winner and an eternal 7th grader and is totally fine with it. Willow collided with Jesus and He radically changed her life and now lives to tell everyone else about Him. Willow lives in Bellingham, Washington with her husband of twenty years and her two amazing kiddos. She speaks about God's love at camps, retreats, churches, and other gatherings, in addition to her work as Founder and Director of Collide.*

Michelle Holladay, Content Contributor   *Michelle believes passionately in God's word and loves helping others discover how relevant the Bible is to our everyday lives. Her ideal day would be spent on a warm beach with a good book. One day, she blinked and her two children were grown, but being a mom will always be her favorite job, one she has happily shared with her husband of over 25 years. We are so grateful for Michelle's love of God's word that guided her to help shape, research and edit the writing and content portion of this study.*

Lindsey Kiniry, Graphic Designer   *Lindsey is a rodeo wrangler, a taxi driver, a chaos manager, and a really terrible chef all rolled into one most days. Though she might seem like the life of the party, this secretly shy gal loves to connect with people one-on-one in a quiet space. Lindsey has a husband, 3 kids, 2 cats, a dog and 8 chickens. Her most favorite moments are in creating something and handing Jesus the paint brush. And boy are we glad that Lindsey does because God continues to use her gifts and did so to create the art in this study that so beautifully draws us into Him.*

Anna Kuttel, Project Manager   *Anna seeks to be authentic by entering into others' joy, hurt, and mess. Anna's background is composed of such seemingly paradoxical passions and experiences as anthropology and interior design, real estate and nonprofit, all of which have shaped her into a continually learning-and-growing wife, a mom of two strong and joyful young boys, and a Collide staff extraordinaire. We are ever thankful to Anna for the way she thinks, organizes, administrates and keeps us all in line- this project needed her gifts to make dreams become reality!*

Kristen Behrends, Content Contributor   *Kristen lives her life by telling the the truth, cultivating real relationships, and leaning into God's plans, even when they're uncomfortable. Though an introvert by nature, Kristen's passion is people, and in loving them she finds meaning for her life. Kristen and her husband live in Bellingham where they enjoy hiking, camping, traveling, and adventuring outdoors. Kristen helps shape and lead our Collide events, which have in turn greatly shaped these studies. We are so grateful for her hardwork and faithfulness!*